A powerful witness to the place of prayer ... friendly daily discipline to introduce you...

—**Thomas W. Gillespie**, President Emeritus, Princeton Theological Seminary

The concept of *Your 100 Days of Prayer* is inspired, and can only accomplish great things for our nation and the Kingdom of God if we'll all cooperate and implement it. The Lord is waiting to see if we have the courage and the desire. He is able.

—**Pat Boone**, singer, actor, producer, author, and motivational speaker

Conversing with our Father in prayer is critical to spiritual growth. In *Your 100 Day Prayer*, John Snyder provides very practical and diverse meditations that will most certainly enhance the reader's prayer life and set the tone for daily living that is focused on God.

—**Rick Dempsey**, senior vice president, Walt Disney Studios

In today's internet age of instant gratification, it's all too easy for Christians to "want it now" and expect the Lord to instantly honor Matthew 7:7—"Ask and it will be given to you . . ." John Snyder's excellent book provides a beautiful pathway to journal our 100 days of focused prayer as we are transformed in the process.

—**David Pack**, Saddleback Church / Orange County, California, Grammy-winning recording artist & music producer

When you're faced with a mountain you can't climb alone, you need more than friendly advice! In this amazing and transforming book, John Snyder takes you on a life-changing journey through 100 days of personal prayer as you follow Jesus' command to ask, seek, and knock. Whether you have a special need or you want a more consistent, meaningful prayer time with God, *Your 100 Day Prayer* gives you daily practical guidance, hope, and encouragement. This is definitely a must-read for ALL Christians!

—**Gregg Bissonette**, Grammy winning musician, drummer

If you already enjoy a daily, satisfying prayer life, don't read this book. But if you're looking for something to stimulate you to become more faithful and systematic, John Snyder's *Your 100 Day Prayer* offers you an opportunity to focus on talking to God daily and making it an ongoing habit.

—**Cecil Murphey,** author or co-author of more than 100 books including *90 Minutes in Heaven* and *Gifted Hands: The Ben Carson Story*

John Snyder has taken a chapter out of his own life and made it available to all of us . . . *Your 100 Day Prayer* is an incredibly practical and powerful tool for any individual or family who desires to develop and strengthen their prayer life.

—**Matt Kees,** director, Christian Musician Summit conferences, and music producer

In this 100-day pilgrimage, Dr. Snyder has woven four great Christian traditions together—daily scripture reading, devotional insight, prayer, and journaling. You cannot practice these disciplines faithfully and emerge unchanged. I think that you will find when the journey has ended, that God has been your guide and your destination.

—**Dr. Ed Ewart,** MOO Church, Mission Viejo, California

YOUR 100 DAY PRAYER

THE TRANSFORMING POWER
OF ACTIVELY WAITING ON GOD

JOHN I. SNYDER

THOMAS NELSON
Since 1798

NASHVILLE   DALLAS   MEXICO CITY   RIO DE JANEIRO

Published in Nashville, Tennessee, by Thomas Nelson. Thomas Nelson is a trademark of Thomas Nelson, Inc.

Thomas Nelson, Inc., titles may be purchased in bulk for educational, business, fund-raising, or sales promotional use. For information, please e-mail SpecialMarkets@ThomasNelson.com.

Library of Congress Cataloging-in-Publication Data

Snyder, John, 1946–
   Your 100 day prayer : the transforming power of actively waiting on God / John I. Snyder.
      p. cm.
Includes bibliographical references and index.
ISBN 978-1-4002-0340-6 (alk. paper)
1. Meditations. I. Title. II. Title: Your hundred day prayer.
BV4832.3.S654 2011
242'.2—dc22

                                                                                    2011015587

Printed in the United States of America

11 12 13 14 15 16 QG 6 5 4 3 2 1

To my wife, Shirin, and daughters, Sarah and Stephanie, with much love and gratitude

CONTENTS

THE SILENT HEAVEN

WHEN GOD SAYS NO

GOD OF THE LAST MINUTE

START DATE

_____

MY PRAYER REQUEST

_____

_____

_____

_____

_____

A PRAYER TO BEGIN

Lord, as I embark on this journey of prayer, come and banish from my heart every last trace of self-reliance and captivate my mind with the truth that you are sufficient for my every need, great or small. Transform me by increasing my confidence in you, in all your extravagant forgiveness and mercy, and strengthen my trembling knees in the face of trouble. Cause my loved ones and me to emerge from this season of prayer with a fresh vision of your glory, a new and lasting fearlessness, and a renewed devotion to your purpose, for Jesus' sake. Amen.

HOW TO USE THIS BOOK

Lord, teach us to pray.

—LUKE 11:1

As Christians, we pray because we are instructed to. It comes on the authority of both the Old and New Testaments. We're taught that without prayer and dependence on the Father and the Son, we'll fail. We have no hope of getting through this life or of ever accomplishing anything for Jesus Christ without him. Jesus even tell us, "Apart from me you can do nothing" (John 15:5).

This book is intended as a guide to your own 100-day prayer, where you will bring your issue before God every day for this 100-day period. Each entry begins with a passage from Scripture and ends with a brief preparation for prayer for that day. After your prayer, you can enter any thoughts, notes, or insights as God reveals them to you in your personal time with him.

So then, how are we to pray? Jesus answers that question too. He spells it out in what we know as "The Lord's Prayer," found in both Matthew 6 and Luke 11. This is not really the

Lord's Prayer. It isn't the prayer that Jesus himself prayed—it's actually the prayer he taught his disciples to pray. So we could call it the Disciples' Prayer. Jesus never needed to say things like "forgive us our sins," because he didn't have any to forgive.

The real Lord's Prayer was recorded in the Garden of Gethsemane just before his arrest. It's made up of three parts:

1. "Your will be done,"
2. "Your will be done," and
3. "Your will be done."

Even though he didn't pray the Disciples' Prayer, we can pray his. In the Disciples' Prayer, Jesus teaches us how to pray. The basic outline looks like this:

Our Father in heaven . . .

We come to God the Father with a sense of complete trust and dependency, just as a small child approaches his or her father. We are encouraged to see God as "Abba" (the Aramaic word for "Papa" or "Daddy").

Forgive us our debts . . .

With this sense of intimacy and total reliance, we come with confession (openness regarding our sins and failures with no attempt to hide them or make excuses for them). We present our praise and thanks for who he is and what he has already done for us.

Lead us not into temptation, but deliver us from evil . . .

Finally, we present to him all the things we want him to do. We can ask anything of him we want to, anything at all. If he thinks that what we ask for is good for us and in accordance with his perfect will, we'll have it. We can ask for health, healing, rescue, a mate, a career, or even a new Lamborghini! The worst that can happen is God can say no. If it's a no, then that means it's not the best thing for us. How bad could that be?

So let's put aside any false humility or pride and come before God with boldness, asking for the moon. Remember, we're coming not to our employer but to the Creator of the universe, who wants to be seen as our heavenly Father and who has our best interests at heart.

INTRODUCTION

When do people pray? Normally it's when they want or need something and think God can bring it to them. We pray for other reasons, too, such as worship or thanksgiving, but probably most of our prayers are to ask God for help, protection, or guidance. When things are particularly serious, we give ourselves to a time of extended prayer until something concrete happens.

This book is a guide to lead you through a 100-day period of prayer as you face a crisis or problem of greater than normal difficulty. It's offered as both an encouragement and a guide to sustained petition. It already has made a remarkable difference to the many who have tried it. It's most effective when carried out by a group of people committed to praying together because, as most of us have discovered, it's just hard to keep on praying by ourselves for something every day for any length of time. Even under normal circumstances, too many distractions and interruptions tend to take us away from our prayer times.

The 100-day prayer is simply a way of bringing before God major issues, challenges, concerns, or transitions in our lives. There's really nothing magic about a hundred days, it's just that my family and I settled on that span of time as a solid period of concentrated prayer and intercession. It could have been ninety or one-hundred-and-twenty days. The intent is only that we bring before God the same issue each day for that period of time. This isn't something overly involved or impossible to sustain—only a few minutes of prayer *every* day. It's striving more for consistency than length of time in prayer.

Our family prayer time lasts only about five to seven minutes a day, whenever we have a chance to be together, any time of the day, but it's usually about the same time every day. It has been especially helpful in the past when we were faced with major problems or life decisions, and for some reason God has always chosen to honor it. Usually not right on the hundredth day, but shortly thereafter and often even earlier.

None of this is purely our idea. It comes straight from the teaching of Jesus: we are supposed to keep on asking, keep on seeking, and keep on knocking if we're to expect things from our heavenly Father. "Ask and it will be given to you; seek and you will find; knock and the door will be opened to you. For everyone who asks receives; he who seeks finds; and to him who knocks, the door will be opened" (Matt. 7:7–8). Apparently, this sustained, stubborn, never-give-up spirit of prayer is not so much to persuade God to give us what we want but, rather, to transform us in the process.

Give yourself to this 100-day spiritual discipline, and you will reap the benefits of it. Only let God in his perfect wisdom be the judge of exactly what he chooses those benefits to be and when he chooses to grant them. When all is said and done, the conclusion of every one of our prayers should be, "Even though I've made it perfectly clear what I want, nevertheless . . . your will be done."

In the Beginning

*In the beginning God created the heavens and the
earth. Now the earth was formless and empty,
darkness was over the surface of the deep, and the
Spirit of God was hovering over the waters.*

−GENESIS 1:1−2

Sometimes the imagery used in the Bible tells us more than
the words themselves. The very first two verses of Genesis
are a perfect example of this. As God began to create the world
we live in, the Hebrew writer portrayed the Spirit of God as
"hovering over" the unformed and unruly mass, much like a
mother bird fluttering over her brood. The picture here is the
very careful and loving attention God gives to his creation—
protecting, shaping, and guiding its development. In other
words, there's no room for chance or randomness. Everything
is under his control.

As God's Spirit hovers, he extracts from the chaos perfect
order, boundaries, and purpose. This appears to be the job
description of the Holy Spirit from day one up to this very day
in our lives. As he continually hovers over all our chaos and disorder—our pain, uncertainty of our future, betrayal, financial
challenges, disorder, deceit, and fear—he brings out of them
the ordered design that he wants for us and that he intended
from the very beginning of the world.

If there is any short summary or basic message we can extract
from the Bible's story of creation, it's this: *God is in charge.* He's
in charge of everything, all the time, and forever. We aren't.

What greater comfort could there be for us? God is with us. Let's hold on to the promise—Emmanuel, God with us. He will rescue and save us.

TODAY'S PRAYER

Ask the Holy Spirit to sweep into your heart and mind, to bring order, peace, and purpose into your need and request.

TODAY'S PROGRESS

_____

_____

_____

_____

_____

_____

_____

_____

_____

_____

_____

_____

Don't Worry

Therefore I tell you, do not worry about your life, what
you will eat or drink; or about your body, what you will
wear. . . . But seek first his kingdom and his righteousness,
and all these things will be given to you as well.

–MATTHEW 6:25, 33

One of the most consistent themes in the New Testament is the encouragement—even the command—not to worry. About anything! It's forbidden. Anxiety has no place in the life of faith because any kind of worry is out of touch with reality. The presence of worry indicates a low level of trust in God, and a high level of trust in God will invariably result in a reduction of worry.

Jesus really does want us to be very low on the worry scale and very high on the peace and joy scale, benefits provided only through trusting implicitly in God. The apostle Paul reiterates the point when he says that we should not be anxious about anything but instead simply make our requests known to God (Phil. 4:5–6).

Sounds simple and clear enough. But why does this seem so impossible to us, and why is trust so hard to find? Jesus gives us the answer: it happens only when we put the kingdom of God first and seek it above anything else on earth. When we wake up every morning and say, "Today, Lord, with your help, I'm going to put you first and seek your perfect will in everything I do," we'll find worry slowly beginning to fade as we stare down every situation with trust in God's providence and goodwill.

No, it won't happen magically or overnight (nothing does), but it will happen. That's the testimony of millions of believers through the centuries. German missionary George Mueller struggled for years to feed hundreds of hungry orphans each day without a regular income, until the day came when, he said, "worry and I parted ways." He simply discovered on the basis of his own long-term experience that God is faithful every day and that worry not only is an enormous waste of time and energy but is also unrealistic. It's out of place in a life of mature faith.

To be sure, it takes all of us time to get this, but in time we will. It's better to get there as early as possible because every day we fill up with anxiety just makes life much harder than it needs to be. So put God and his kingdom first, and let him bring to you, as you sleep, all the things the rest of the world works feverishly through the night trying to acquire.

TODAY'S PRAYER

Go to God humbly and ask him to reveal the secret places of worry and anxiety that surround you and your need.

TODAY'S PROGRESS

_____

_____

_____

_____

_____

_____

Good out of Evil

*You intended to harm me, but God intended it for good to
accomplish what is now being done, the saving of many lives.*

–GENESIS 50:20

This statement near the end of the incredible story of Joseph is
one of the most amazing truths in the Bible. It summarizes
the entire history of faith—yours, mine, and everyone else's. It
ties up all the loose ends of human life lived under the umbrella
of God's grace and mercy. It speaks of God's mysterious ability
to take any and all evil, all malicious intent, and turn it on its
head. It's the practical outworking of what is said in the very
first verses of Genesis about the work of the Holy Spirit—that
God's Spirit hovers over us and draws order and purpose out of
our own chaos and disorder, just as he did at the beginning of
creation.

God takes every malevolent thing aimed at us by others and
deliberately exploits it for his purposes and our good. People
may imagine that their cruel or self-serving plans are working
perfectly, but at the right moment God reveals that he stepped
in early, wrote a different conclusion to the play, and brought us
from the place of their curse into the place of his blessing. As the
great Scriptwriter of history, he reserves the right to change all
minor plots into his great plot. So he remains the author, director, and main actor of every play on his earth.

What a reason to stay positive in every single situation in
life! Try to imagine how God is actively working in your life
to create exits for the traps and corners thought up for you by

someone else. Think of the fact that every plot hatched by your adversaries to entrap or destroy you is being turned into a blessing by your heavenly Father. These rescues and reversals may not be evident early in the game (it wasn't to Joseph either), but they will be clear at the end. Anywhere along the line of his story, Joseph could have stopped and concluded that God was against him, had forgotten all about him, and tossed him aside. Yet when the last chapter is written and all the loose ends are tied together, God's providential hand becomes evident in every detail of the story.

And that's the good news for us. God is acting behind the scenes even when we may not recognize his presence, but he's there nonetheless, and he determines the final scene of the play. Thankfully, it's in our favor.

TODAY'S PRAYER

Do you see any external barriers or enemies between you and your need? Go to God and ask for his perspective so that it can inform and transform yours.

TODAY'S PROGRESS

_____

_____

_____

_____

_____

_____

DAY 4

He Heals the Brokenhearted

He heals the brokenhearted and binds up their wounds.

-PSALM 147:3

What's so hopeful about this kind of statement in the Bible is that God's involvement with us isn't so "spiritual" and heavenly that it has no earthly good.

This is really where the rubber meets the road: God is very present with us in our broken-heartedness, disillusionments, despair, and wounded spirits. These painful experiences—those that go deep into our hearts and psyches and daily eat away at the center of our being—are what occupy too many of our days.

It's not just the great conflicts on the global or national level or the issues that appear on the evening news that God is concerned about—the small and the highly personal and intimate issues also attract his loving attention. He meets us where we are, not just where we ought to be. He wants to heal our deep hurts and bind up our hidden wounds—those not evident to anyone else—because he cares about such things and intends to do something about them. It's in the soil of this well-grounded hope that we are able to trust and grow.

If sometimes God doesn't heal our wounds the very moment we ask him, it's not because he isn't concerned; it's because he intends to grow us through them. That might even be the reason they were allowed to come our way in the first place. If God is really in charge of everything all the time, then he's in charge of this as well. And don't forget, there will come a day when such things are no longer even a memory:

> He will wipe every tear from their eyes. There will be no more death or mourning or crying or pain, for the old order of things has passed away. (Rev. 21:4)

TODAY'S PRAYER

Are there places in your heart and soul that feel so wounded that your prayer request feels out of reach *because of you*? Ask God to give you his eternal perspective on your development as a person of faith.

TODAY'S PROGRESS

_____

_____

_____

_____

_____

_____

_____

_____

_____

_____

The Father's House

Do not let your hearts be troubled. Trust in God; trust also in me. In my Father's house are many rooms; if it were not so, I would have told you. I am going there to prepare a place for you. And if I go and prepare a place for you, I will come back and take you to be with me that you also may be where I am.

–JOHN 14:1–3

This wonderful passage is even better than it first appears. It has a double reference, both of which are extremely good news for us. On the one hand, it seems to refer to the place Jesus is about to prepare for us by going to the cross—a place in the Father's house that he alone enjoyed before coming to live among us. He had perfect fellowship with God the Father long before his incarnation as a human being, a unique place of love and intimacy he is about to share with all his followers.

In other words, by going to the cross and paying for our sins, he creates a "dwelling place" for us to enjoy right now, today, not someday in the indeterminate future. We can have that place with the Father and in the Father's house that Jesus had and now has. We can live where he lives, close to the Father's heart.

But it means even more. Not only can we have that abiding place of nearness to God right now so that we can pray, "Abba Father" ("Papa" or something close to that), but we will be safely at home in the Father's house for eternity when this "preliminary life" is done. So the benefits of Jesus' death on the cross are for right now as well as in the future; he has provided all the privileges of being in the family of God today, tomorrow, and forever.

Can it get any better than that? Once we grasp this sure truth, it begins to squeeze out all despair, depression, darkness, and negative thinking. The joy of this may not happen overnight (it's not magic), but it will grow real as the way gets brighter and brighter as we walk the long walk of faith.

Life teaches us this lesson: we can get through anything when we know what the end looks like. Thankfully, God has given us a clear picture of what our destiny actually is, sealed with his proven promise and illustrated ahead of time by Jesus' resurrection.

TODAY'S PRAYER

Ask God to fill your heart with the joy and security of a sure destination. Then think of the nature of your need in light of God's eternal plans for you.

TODAY'S PROGRESS

_____

_____

_____

_____

_____

_____

_____

Ever the Same

*Sing joyfully to the LORD, you righteous; it is fitting for the
upright to praise him. Praise the LORD with the harp; make
music to him on the ten-stringed lyre. Sing to him a new
song; play skillfully, and shout for joy. For the word of the
LORD is right and true; he is faithful in all he does.*

–PSALM 33:1–4

Can you think of any reason to sing joyfully at this very moment? If something really bad just happened to you, you probably can't. But there is a reason to be joyful whether you feel like it or not. In fact, if we wait until we feel full of joyful praise to God before we actually do praise him, we might be waiting until Armageddon! There's always something that will keep us from being joyful.

That's why we need to learn a lesson from those who have gone before us. We praise God, sing to him a new song, and shout for joy just because he is who he is, because his word is right and true, and because he is faithful in all he does. We don't need any more reasons than these.

Praise is simply acknowledging who and what God is. We offer praise on the grounds of his worthiness of it. We may be staring at the magnificence of the Grand Canyon while at the same time feeling sick with the flu, but we still find ourselves saying, "What an awesome sight!" So it is with God. We might be going through a tough time or not even want to get out of bed in the morning, but we can still manage to thank God and offer him praise for who he is and all that he has done and will do.

Once we get the full picture of who God is (it doesn't happen in one day), what he's done for us, what awaits us, and how faithful he has been and will continue to be, the praise part gets much easier. Time and experience teach us the discipline of praising God in spite of the things going on around us or within us. Whatever they may be, they're temporary, while God's trustworthiness and faithfulness are permanent. Our feelings come and go, but God's word and purpose are ever the same.

So we can stay positive and expectant even when we don't feel like it. Maturity in faith comes when we can say in all honesty, "I don't feel positive and upbeat today because it seems like things couldn't be worse. But I can keep my eyes on the compass of God's ever-steady character and true word. I can know that he controls all things, in good weather or bad. The storm can't destroy me because he won't let it. I can't see it yet, but I'm convinced there's a safe harbor ahead—he promised it."

TODAY'S PRAYER

Ask God to give you the extraordinary, what you can't create for yourself—the ability to praise him for his faithfulness in meeting your need even before your need is felt.

TODAY'S PROGRESS

Finish the Race

Forgetting what is behind and straining toward what is
ahead, I press on toward the goal to win the prize for which
God has called me heavenward in Christ Jesus.

–PHILIPPIANS 3:13–14

If you want to keep going forward, expecting the things you're praying for, waiting patiently for them, and not being brought down by all the negative things of the past, then this passage is written for you. Try to put yourself in the mind of the apostle, who was most likely using imagery from a competitive race. If you want to finish the race and come out victorious at the end, then you'll have to put aside everything bad that's happened along the way.

Paul doesn't mean that we can literally forget the bad, as if we should try to convince ourselves that it didn't really happen or that we can somehow block it all out of our memories or pretend it was some other way. I think he meant only that we aren't to keep the bad in the forefront of our minds, allowing it to shape our decisions and control our lives. He says that we are to focus our attention on the future, to keep our eyes on the finish line with such concentration that nothing else can distract us.

For example, if you're running a hurdle race, you can't afford to think about the hurdle you just hit, the pain in your leg, the person next to you who fell, or the applause, shouting, or cursing coming from the crowds. Your mind must be totally focused on the tape at the finish line. It's not that you're unaware of it all; it's only that you mustn't let yourself be influenced or controlled by any of it. There's something more important that should be occupying your attention.

So it is with all the mistreatment we receive, the mistakes we've made, the slander of our names, the misperceptions, lost relationships, regrets, fraud, deception, and everything else that can come our way in this life. If we're to move ahead successfully and keep on praying effectively, we must not let anything control our decisions or thinking so much that we are thrown off course.

Nothing can derail us in our spiritual lives more quickly than bitterness, guilt, growing hatred, resentments, continual rehearsal of that argument we had, the stupid things we've done, the abuse we received, and all the rest. With God's help, we have to let it go. The only healthy way that can happen is for us to refocus on the goal of glorifying God every time we're tempted to stop and go over it one more time.

TODAY'S PRAYER

Pray that God will show you if any unnecessary concentration on your past is hindering (or preventing) your need from being met.

TODAY'S PROGRESS

_____

_____

_____

_____

_____

_____

Wait for the Lord

Wait for the LORD; be strong and take heart
and wait for the LORD.

–PSALM 27:14

If ever there was some tough advice to swallow, this is it: "Wait for the LORD." But we don't want to wait. We want what we want, and we want it right now . . . or no later than next Tuesday! That's what it means to be a modern person in our fast-moving, high-tech world. We don't tolerate slow computers, slow service, or slow traffic. It's just not in our blood.

But that's not God's way. He doesn't mind waiting, and he doesn't mind our waiting either. In fact, he goes out of his way sometimes just to put us in situations where we can do nothing but wait. Been there? Are you there now? If so, cheer up! The psalmist tells us to be strong and take heart and wait for the Lord. If anything matures our faith, it's this—waiting for the Lord to act when no other power can help.

Read any Christian biography and what do you find? Normally, we see that the experience of the growing believer is punctuated with frequent and sometimes extended periods of waiting. Waiting for what? Waiting for God to step in and do what we can't. It's in the waiting and hoping, waiting and praying, waiting and expecting, that our faith stretches or takes quantum leaps upward.

Have you ever wondered why so often in history God waits until the last minute to step in and help his people? Because it's in that last second, in the fifty-ninth minute of the eleventh hour, that he gets his best work done. That's where we stretch and grow. If God answered our prayers the very moment we first prayed, we wouldn't grow a single millimeter. No, it's the waiting that keeps us dependent on him as we experience his total trustworthiness. Praise God for his mercy in not acting too soon!

TODAY'S PRAYER

Plan to wait on God. Ask him to accomplish exactly what he wants for you in the process of bringing the things you want and need.

TODAY'S PROGRESS

Break the Circuit

Do not be overcome by evil, but overcome evil with good.

–ROMANS 12:21

This would be only a nice religious saying if it weren't for the powerful life principle embedded in it. Few seriously doubt that evil exists in the world, and those who do aren't taken seriously. The only real question for us is what to do about it.

We aren't talking so much about forming national or international policy here (although it's not excluded)—rather we're speaking of what you and I can do in daily, real-life situations, responding to evil when it gets really personal.

Evil is like an electric current. It flows from one person to another when the circuit is closed, and it stops flowing when the circuit is open. How do we open the circuit? We don't allow it to move through us to the next person. If we hear unsubstantiated, destructive gossip about our neighbor, we don't pass it on. It stops with us. If someone insults or wounds us, we don't insult back or pass on our anger to another innocent person, become hard to live with, or kick the dog when we get home. In other words, we break the circuit. We don't allow it to keep going.

For truly positive living and to maintain a positive outlook, we must not allow evil behavior to change us into the likeness of those who seem to love it and live for it. End it right where it strikes. A calm or kind word goes much farther than a quick and clever (or usually not-so-clever) retort, as good as that may feel at the moment.

On a lesser scale, try giving a gift to a grouchy neighbor or an extra tip to a surly waiter and see what happens. More often than not, it'll change the situation entirely. And even if it doesn't, it changes us. These good-for-bad exchanges turn the tables, put us in charge of the situation, surprise the aggressor, and contribute to the general peace around us.

TODAY'S PRAYER

Bring to God in total honesty the evil that besets you, and ask him to reveal how you can break the circuit and end its power over you or your neighbor.

TODAY'S PROGRESS

_____

_____

_____

_____

_____

_____

_____

_____

_____

_____

Disturbing the Heart of God

In all their distress he too was distressed, and the angel of
his presence saved them. In his love and mercy he redeemed
them; he lifted them up and carried them all the days of old.

–ISAIAH 63:9

Does God care what I'm going through?"
Have you ever said that? If you haven't, it's very likely that you will someday. When you do, try to remember this: God not only knows everything that's happening in every square inch of his creation, he knows every thought of every heart at every moment.

And there's more. God not only knows every thought and emotion, but he actually enters into our own distress with us and feels what we feel. Our distress causes distress in God. Think about it for a moment. The Creator of the universe, a universe too immense even to imagine, is not only aware of our deepest emotion but also feels it with us. Our pain can disturb the heart of God.

This point is made clear in Isaiah. The people of Israel richly deserved what they were going through because they had been so disobedient and rebellious, even wicked. They had totally and completely failed to act like God's people. But he felt no pleasure in punishing them. He was (and still is) like the loving parent who feels the distress of the child under discipline.

And it's not as if they blew it just once and straightened out.

They fell time after time, rebelled repeatedly, turned away from God in the foolish pursuit of selfish and silly things. There was absolutely no reason that God would or should stick with his people. There never has been, except for one quality of his own character—he's loyal and loving to the max.

We can be thankful that the people of Israel behaved as they did because it gives us hope that God remains faithful to all those he loves, even when we aren't faithful to him. It's a reassurance to us when we feel that we haven't done much better.

So here is the reason to remain positive: In his love and mercy he redeemed them; he lifted them up and carried them for the rest of their days. It had nothing to do with the quality of their performance. God stayed true to his people just because of his love and mercy and for no other reason.

TODAY'S PRAYER

As you pray for your need, keep in the front of your mind that God not only is ever-mindful of your need but also—as the good, patient, and forgiving parent he is—feels your distress.

TODAY'S PROGRESS

_____

_____

_____

_____

_____

_____

Pressed but Not Crushed

We are hard pressed on every side, but not crushed;
perplexed, but not in despair; persecuted, but not
abandoned; struck down, but not destroyed. We always
carry around in our body the death of Jesus, so that the life
of Jesus may also be revealed in our body. For we who are
alive are always being given over to death for Jesus' sake, so
that his life may be revealed in our mortal body.

—2 CORINTHIANS 4:8–11

We know from this and other passages in Paul's letters, and in Luke's various reports in Acts, that Paul didn't live a life of carefree ease. He was beaten multiple times, shipwrecked more than once, left adrift at sea, betrayed, falsely accused, imprisoned, and pursued by enemies his entire Christian life. According to tradition, he was executed by beheading in or around Rome in the first century.

But he didn't really expect anything different. This was exactly what he was told would happen if he chose to live a life in Christ Jesus. And this is exactly what we might expect as well if we choose to follow the Son of God.

But look at the payback! Yes, terrible things might be happening to us, but how else are we to experience the amazing things that come as a result of all our trials and sorrow? How else will others see the life of Jesus being revealed in us? There is no other way we can witness to God's rescuing power in our lives. Miracles happen where they're needed! And in the midst of our troubles, we find Christ's presence and delivering power.

If all we experience in this life is more and more ease, increasing luxury, and prosperity, then we'll be total strangers to the many sorts of rescues, happy restorations, and healings that come to the people of God.

It's through seeing God work in our lives that we come to the solid conviction that there really is a magnificent, extravagant, over-the-top resurrection life at the end. We come to this confidence by means of all the little resurrections and reversals of fortune that come our way on the journey of faith.

Thank God for his daily deliverances and faithfulness! We can keep on praying because it makes a difference.

TODAY'S PRAYER

Consider what you're praying and waiting for in the light of what God is doing right now in bringing you to a higher level of faith. Ask God for eyes of faith.

TODAY'S PROGRESS

_____

_____

_____

_____

_____

_____

_____

The Lord Is My Shepherd

The Lord is my shepherd, I shall not be in want.

-PSALM 23:1

This sentence has been repeated in our culture and in our churches so many times that it's gone the way of all overly familiar words. If we hear something often enough, it tends to lose its force.

This is the Old Testament version of what Jesus expressed in the Lord's Prayer: "Give us our daily bread." Although it is said in dozens of different ways throughout the Bible, the point is the same: If we look to God for our needs, he'll supply them. If God is our shepherd, we won't get lost or end up in oblivion or final desperation or destitution.

Does this mean that we'll never have hard times or that we'll never experience suffering, hunger, or material shortages? No, of course not. Human history thoroughly refutes this. Christians in every part of the world and in every generation have experienced all sorts of want and deprivation. Prison and labor camps, squalid refugee cities, persecution, and inner-city poverty are not the fate merely of unbelievers. It's bad theology (and gross dishonesty) to make people think that if you just "come to Jesus and accept him as your personal savior," then from now on everything's going to be perfect.

This has never been true before, and it isn't now. So where's the reason to be positive in our prayer and expectation? The passage here from David is a song. It was to express a relationship between God and us. He is the shepherd, and we are the sheep.

He'll lead us in the right way so that our ultimate safety will be guaranteed. Nothing can harm us in any permanent way, and nothing can lead us so far off the path that we'll never get back home to the fold. As a general rule, he'll supply us with the practical needs of life even though we'll pass through lean times. He'll keep us in his hands even when danger is all around us.

We might even perish (eventually it will happen one way or another), but even in death, he's still our shepherd. We'll never have to face the great black abyss alone. Even there, he'll be by our side to lead us, for there is no place in this world or the next that he's unfamiliar with or where we are beyond his leading and protection. One thing we can be sure of is this: Even if God allows us to appear lost for a season (or short of food or housing for a time, or alone and without friends), it's not even a remote possibility to be outside the realm of his loving care and guidance. In the end, we can't really ever lose.

TODAY'S PRAYER

Ask God to help you let go of your shock at the fact that you really have this need. Pray that he'll put in your heart the song of faith in the midst of it.

TODAY'S PROGRESS

_____

_____

_____

_____

_____

Nothing's Impossible

*Jesus looked at them and said, "With man this is impossible,
but not with God; all things are possible with God."*

−MARK 10:27

The word *impossible* isn't part of God's vocabulary. It's a word we thought up on our own, and we think it carries lots of weight. But it does so only when we subtract God from the formula. If there's no God, the kind of God portrayed in the Bible, then we would have every right to think that there are all kinds of impossible things in the world.

But it makes perfect sense that if the God of the Bible exists, then there's nothing, literally nothing, that's impossible. By definition, God excludes the realm of the impossible. Water into wine? No problem. Quelling a storm? Easy. Bringing dead bodies back to life? Done. That's the paradigm we need to use when viewing life's problems and fears.

Just look at the record. Who are the people who have accomplished astonishing things in history? Those who have refused to believe that certain things are impossible.

Who taught us that powered flight was possible? Two Bible students named Orville and Wilbur Wright, who were convinced that we could fly in spite of all the experts who said it was impossible.

Who were the first scientists in modern history? People like Copernicus, Newton, Kepler, and Galileo, who believed that an all-powerful God was really there and that the Bible gives a true account of him.

Who established against all odds the most extensive system of hospitals, schools, orphanages, feeding stations, and refugee camps in the history of the world? People like Henri Dunant, Florence Nightingale, Gladys Aylward, William Booth, and Amy Carmichael, who knew that with God, nothing is ever impossible.

In fact, it could be said that the job description of Christians in the world has always been to attempt the impossible with God's help. What more motivation could God give us to help us get up in the morning with a view toward the positive and with great confidence in prayer?

TODAY'S PRAYER

Ask God to drive out entirely from your mind the slightest thought that your need, no matter how profound, approaches the impossible.

TODAY'S PROGRESS

_____

_____

_____

_____

_____

_____

_____

The Master Plan

The LORD brings death and makes alive; he brings down
to the grave and raises up. The LORD sends poverty and
wealth; he humbles and he exalts.

–1 SAMUEL 2:6–7

This is just one of many places where the Bible affirms that it is God alone who is in charge of history—the world's and ours. Job, for example, says, "I know that you can do all things; no plan of yours can be thwarted" (Job 42:2). The biblical writers were all on the same page when it came to believing that God is in control of all things and that nothing can happen that he doesn't first review and allow. He's never in the position of wringing his hands in confusion; he's never surprised at what occurs on earth; he's never wondering what to do next. Beware of any view of God that sees him as only the reactor to what people do, rather than the principal actor on the stage.

Whether life or death, success or failure, rising or falling of individuals or nations, everything is in his hands. He takes everything into account, to the last detail, before it happens. The rampant idea today that the Devil makes the bad things happen and God makes the good things happen is extremely bad theology. What kind of God would that be? It would make God and Satan approximate equals, each one in charge of a part of the world.

No, this isn't remotely what the Bible teaches about God. God and God alone is the one who has a master plan for the ages, and he intends to stick with his plan regardless of whether we cooperate with him or not. He allows us to exercise our wills, to serve him or oppose him, to love him or hate him, but in the end it will come out just the way he intends it to come out.

Of course, all this is not good news to those who have plans to do things their way in disregard of God's will, but it's very good news if we want to serve and obey him. It means that whatever anyone wants to do against God or to harm us will be in vain. Even if it appears to be successful for a season, in the end it will be for nothing. No evil will triumph. But everyone who serves God faithfully and joyfully can know that God's ultimate plan of the ages will be the last one standing.

We can move through this life without despair because we can refer all things to God, knowing not only that he is in total charge of everything but also that his will is good and that it's steeply tilted in our direction.

TODAY'S PRAYER

During this period of prayerful waiting, bring to God your entire view of life and ask him to reshape it according to his eternal plan. Then repeatedly lift up your need to the heavenly Father in the light of his good purpose that cannot ever fail.

TODAY'S PROGRESS

_____

_____

_____

_____

_____

Saltiness

*You are the salt of the earth. But if the salt loses its saltiness,
how can it be made salty again? It is no longer good for
anything, except to be thrown out and trampled by men.*

—MATTHEW 5:13

Just imagine what Jesus is saying to us here. He's giving us
our job description, of course, but also something far more.
He's telling us not so much what to do, but who we are. We may
think, *Why be positive in a downward-moving, decaying, negative,
dangerous world?* Because of the people Jesus says we are and the
role we're given to play in it.

Salt of the earth? Light of the world? That sounds more like
what Jesus would say *he* was. Yet he's talking about *us*. We're the
ones who are supposed to be salty, tasty, tangy. We're the ones
who are supposed to provide the spice of life to the world. Jesus'
true followers are supposed to be the red-hot chili pepper in the
mix. But how?

It's clearly not because we are so great in and of ourselves.
It's only by the Holy Spirit dwelling in us that any of this is possible. When, and only when, Jesus resides in us and empowers us
can we be the conduit of his preserving and healing saltiness to
others. Only as his light shines through us can we become light
in the darkness to our neighbors and friends—and enemies.

But this is exactly what he's getting at. He will be the light
of the world and the salt of the earth through us. When the
world sees him in us, in our actions and attitudes, then it will
recognize that without him there is no tang to life and no light

to guide us out of the darkness. Then when we are fulfilling this job description, we'll find ourselves saying, "Now I see why we're on this earth. Finally, I understand why I'm here, where I'm going, and what it all means."

TODAY'S PRAYER

Ask the Holy Spirit to reveal to you the important role your need and the answering of it plays in the greater drama of our calling to be salt in the world.

TODAY'S PROGRESS

Wait in Hope

*We wait in hope for the L*ORD*; he is our help
and our shield. In him our hearts rejoice, for
we trust in his holy name.*

–PSALM 33:20–21

Why are there so many places in the Bible where hoping
and waiting are linked together? Well obviously, if we had
what we wanted, we wouldn't be hoping for it. The child hopes
for a new bicycle for Christmas because Christmas hasn't yet
come. But that's not all there is to say about it.

The psalmist waits, but he waits for a sure thing. The word
hope in the Bible doesn't mean what most of us mean when
we use it. It carries with it the sense not of "I sure hope so,"
but rather, "I know that my expectation won't be disappointed."
What the psalmist waits for in absolute unwavering surety is not
that God will give him the new toy *du jour* but that God will
grant the need of the day—help in the time of danger or need
and shelter from the storm.

Of course, God often gives us the things our hearts desire,
but if we have to wait, let's focus our eyes on the ever-faithfulness
of God, who gives us whatever we need to get through our trial
of the moment.

TODAY'S PRAYER

Ask that God grant such an overwhelming sense of his sufficiency for the day that you'll be able to rest in the unshakable

confidence (hope) that whatever he gives you will be the right and best thing.

TODAY'S PROGRESS

_____

_____

_____

_____

_____

_____

_____

_____

_____

_____

_____

_____

_____

_____

Living Our Purpose

For it is God who works in you to will and to act
according to his good purpose.

–PHILIPPIANS 2:13

This sounds like several other passages in Paul's letters because he loves to return to this wonderful theme. Remember, we're not the principal actors on the stage—God is. But he wants us on the stage too, and he loves to be there with us. He chooses to act and work through us as his people, not merely to make us sit quietly in the audience and applaud. God takes us very seriously and wants to accomplish his work in and through us.

He could have done it all some other way, but he has chosen this way. It's part of that astonishing New Covenant promised in the Old Testament (Jer. 31:31–33), now realized in the people of God who make up the church. It is God who now puts his Spirit in us to grant us the desire to do his will, then empowers us to do it, all for his good purpose in the world.

No, we aren't robots, mindlessly moving forward in some sort of hypnotic daze. We are real people who are acting freely for the first time, no longer bound and chained to live as slaves to sin, but set free to think rationally and act in a sane, responsible, and productive way.

This passage is one of those that touch upon that most central of all mysteries in the Bible: the connection between our freedom and God's sovereignty. How do the two work together? The question isn't answered in some nice, neat, simple way because it can't be. The Bible merely affirms that God gets his way and he does so through us. And we probably couldn't understand it if it were explained.

All we really need to know is that we have the joy of living with meaning and purpose in this world and the next, all along being motivated and empowered by the Holy Spirit to do the impossible in a mundane and predictable world. If this doesn't get you going, nothing will!

TODAY'S PRAYER

Ask God for eyes of faith that allow you to see your need from an entirely new point of view. No longer view it merely as something you have to get through. See it as the very thing that God is using to work out his purpose through you.

TODAY'S PROGRESS

_____

_____

_____

_____

_____

_____

_____

_____

_____

When We Feel Forsaken

My God, my God, why have you forsaken me? Why are you so
far from saving me, so far from the words of my groaning?

–PSALM 22:1

Have you ever said something like this before in your prayers? It's the standard human complaint: we've called out to God for help, and yet he doesn't seem to answer.

This psalm describes one of the times when King David felt totally forsaken not only by other people but also by his own God. Enemies abounded on every side. People were just waiting for him to make one wrong move so they could destroy him. Now it seemed to him that even God was against him. He was left on his own, and there was no help. Didn't God promise to deliver him whenever he called out for help?

But here's the reason for hope: if David, one of the top heroes of the Bible, could reach this state of absolute spiritual destitution and sense of abandonment, then there's no big problem when we reach that same place.

And since we know that David's sense of forsakenness was only a misperception and illusion of abandonment, then it's really the same for us. It's all just appearance. We know from reading his other psalms, and from the events of his life recorded in 1 and 2 Samuel, that he was never really forsaken at all.

When Jesus was being crucified on the cross centuries later, these were exactly his words. He felt abandoned by his Father as he took upon himself the weight of the world's sin. We don't know all that was going on here with the only Son of God, the human being in all of history most intimate with God the Father, but we know that he, too, experienced a period of time when he thought all the same things that David did.

What we need to keep in mind is that however the psalm starts out, it is still one of those rescue psalms. As you read, it becomes clear that whatever the thoughts or feelings of David were at first, in the end he knew that it was only illusion:

> For he has not despised or disdained the suffering of the afflicted one; he has not hidden his face from him but has listened to his cry for help. (Ps. 22:24)

It was true of David. It was true of Jesus. It will be just as true for us. David was heard and vindicated, Jesus was raised from the dead on the third day, and we too will see with our own eyes the salvation of God.

TODAY'S PRAYER

Since vindication and rescue are often not immediate, appeal to the Father for that extra measure of waiting, sustaining faith. He is the Author of all faith and can give as much of it as needed before the day breaks.

TODAY'S PROGRESS

_____

_____

_____

_____

_____

Rejoice!

Rejoice in the Lord always. I will say it again: Rejoice! Let your gentleness be evident to all. The Lord is near. Do not be anxious about anything, but in everything, by prayer and petition, with thanksgiving, present your requests to God. And the peace of God, which transcends all understanding, will guard your hearts and your minds in Christ Jesus.

–PHILIPPIANS 4:4–7

This is unusual advice from someone in prison. "Rejoice!" the apostle Paul says repeatedly, and he seems to mean it! What was there in his imprisonment that enabled him to be joyful when most of life's freedoms and privileges had been taken from him?

First of all, he was convinced that God was near him. Probably most of us imagine that God dwells with his Son light years away in heaven and will someday come again from that great distance to take us to himself.

But that was not Paul's understanding. Our *cosmology* (view of the universe) needs to be revised. For him, God and Jesus are near. They aren't billions of miles away, but just inches above our heads. When Jesus came into the world, and even when he ascended to the Father, both he and the Father were viewed by the New Testament writers as our next-door neighbors.

Look at it this way: there's a very porous membrane between us and the ceiling, and all the powers and realities of heaven pass through it. When we pray and God sends us visitations of his Spirit or his angels, they come and go through this mysterious, invisible partition. They move from one dimension to another in just a split second. The Lord is always near, just a breath away.

We are supposed to rejoice because we can offer up our requests to a God who is very near us and because, even before we receive, we can experience the peace of God who shares with us the joy of his presence. So when we pray, we're to pray without anxiety. Our Father knows what we need (and want) and will bring us our bread for today, even if our deepest heart's desires and dreams are still a bit in the distance.

TODAY'S PRAYER

Pray that God will show you in various ways how close to you he really is. Then ask the Spirit to grant the heavenly gift of joy just because God and his kingdom are very near.

TODAY'S PROGRESS

Here for a Reason

I cry out to God Most High, to God, who
fulfills his purpose for me.

–PSALM 57:2

If there's one thing that most completely dispels our despair and daily anxieties in this life, it's the fact that we have a purpose and that this purpose was designed and put into effect long before we ever came on the scene. We're here for a reason. We're not an accident. When this truth reaches deep down inside us and gets a hold of our hearts and imaginations, nothing is ever the same again.

"I have a purpose!" It may take most of a lifetime for this to sink in, but when it does, we see everything in a different light. Every relationship, task, motive, goal, and plan will be reordered around this main life theme. And the greater news is that this purpose fits into a larger plan that goes far beyond our own life span. It was on the drawing board at the creation of the universe, and it will work its way through all of life until this present earth comes to an end, then into the ages to come, stretching into the new heaven and the new earth.

But it gets even better. Not only do we have a purpose in being here, but God himself will fulfill it in and through us. It's not as if we're given a purpose at birth and then told that it's totally up to us to make it happen. That would just be mean! Left to our own resources, how frustrating would it be to try and try, only to find that we couldn't make anything happen?

Most of us have probably already discovered this. We have

some great goal or intent to do something—exercise every day, finish school, quit smoking—but it just doesn't seem to work. We find that things usually don't come out as we thought or hoped they would.

That's where the good news comes in. It's God who has determined our purpose in the first place, and it's God who brings it to pass in his perfect time. If we come to discern, love, and delight in his purpose and learn to work with it and not against it—if our will gets in line with his—then we can't fail.

TODAY'S PRAYER

Continually ask the Author of purpose to unfold what yours is. Rest in the fact that, as it gets clearer day by day, God himself will be the power to bring it to pass.

TODAY'S PROGRESS

_____

_____

_____

_____

_____

_____

_____

_____

First Things First

*Ask and it will be given to you; seek and you will find; knock
and the door will be opened to you. For everyone who asks
receives; he who seeks finds; and to him who knocks, the
door will be opened.*

–MATTHEW 7:7–8

ocation, location, location! This passage comes up right in the
midst of Jesus' teaching on God's kingdom. Jesus instructs
his disciples on the necessity of putting God and his will first
and foremost in our lives. When we get that transaction straight,
then we can begin to live our lives of faith in such a way that the
real stuff happens. We find ourselves asking for truly good and
intelligent things rather than the trivial and silly. We spend more
of our prayer hours in requesting what he wants, not in trying to
build our own kingdoms with more and more selfish things.

When we place God first, instead of being concerned about
ourselves and asking only for our needs and desires, we find
ourselves begging for the rescue of the abused and dispossessed.
It's not that God frowns upon the good things we want and
ask for, it's just that he tends to provide those things as a bonus
when we care as much about our neighbor's welfare as we do
about our own.

Let's put it this way: When the Spirit of Jesus takes up resi-
dence in us at conversion (the first day of real faith), he begins to
sweep the house and straighten it up. We start to value what he
values, want what he wants, see things and people his way, and
live for him instead of for ourselves.

So when we start to pray and ask for things, we'll be asking for those things that are in line with his will, and then we'll see more and more of what we ask for happening in our lives. This is the promise of Jesus. This is what it means to pray in his name.

Jesus is also saying that we should never give up praying. Asking, seeking, and knocking suggest that we stay with it— keep on asking, keep on seeking, and keep on knocking. Don't give up if it doesn't happen by early next week. He likes us to hang in there and press on with our requests. God chooses to take time, to use time, and to act in time (and on time) in carrying out his will.

So there's no reason whatsoever to give up or stop praying or end up in despair, and every reason to stay positive no matter what's happening at the moment to us and around us. God is working out his best plans and purposes for our lives.

TODAY'S PRAYER

Because it's so easy to fool ourselves, ask God to reveal to you whether you're truly putting his kingdom first. And always keep in mind that, for reasons not entirely known to us, he wants us to bring our requests continually before him.

TODAY'S PROGRESS

_____

_____

_____

_____

See for Yourself

In you our fathers put their trust; they trusted and you delivered them. They cried to you and were saved; in you they trusted and were not disappointed.

–PSALM 22:4–5

This sounds like many other statements in the Bible, but there's an important difference here. It says a great deal more about the solid foundation of our faith and gives us another reason to stay hopeful no matter what's going on around us. It affirms once more that God is reliable and that if we trust him we won't be disappointed.

That's good news enough. But that's not all there is. Remember, this is a continuation of the same psalm where David expresses his sense of total abandonment, but then everything changes toward the end. He's not simply saying that since his ancestors believed and trusted in God, so God ought to come and help him too. David is actually saying that since they trusted God and found him faithful, he will also see the faithfulness of God.

It seems to me that David's point is that even though, at the moment, God seems to be absent, this whole thing has been thoroughly road-tested and tried too many times to count. It's been found to be true over every generation and can be found to be true in this one and all the rest to follow. Now it's had over four thousand years to be tried and tested in the crucible of human experience and has been found absolutely true in the lives of millions of real people in real life.

So we should always be looking on the bright side because we have every reason to. It's actually irrational not to. However things may look at the moment, we can rely on the time-tested confidence that God is in charge of history and that in his time and way, according to his own plan, he will bring about his good purpose.

And if you have trouble believing the thousands of years of human experience and testimony that prove all this is true, then don't believe it. Just try it for yourself. You'll see. David summarized the trustworthiness of God not by saying, "Stop doubting and just take my word for it," but rather by saying, "Taste and see that the LORD is good" (Ps. 34:8).

TODAY'S PRAYER

Ask the Lord to impress this upon your mind so powerfully that you can't get away from it: all history cries out that God is the Ruler of all things great and small. However bleak it may look at the moment, he's actually on his way, bringing the good news with him.

TODAY'S PROGRESS

_____

_____

_____

_____

_____

How to Save a Life

*Then he called the crowd to him along with his disciples
and said: "If anyone would come after me, he must deny
himself and take up his cross and follow me. For whoever
wants to save his life will lose it, but whoever loses his life
for me and for the gospel will save it."*

−MARK 8:34–35

Here's one of life's best-kept secrets: If we try to fulfill ourselves by ourselves, or to realize our dreams on our own steam and by our own personal plans ("save" our lives), we'll fail in the attempt. But if we give up our lives and hand them over to our Creator, asking him to have his perfect will even over our own ("lose" our lives), we'll find to our surprise that we're fulfilled by it.

This is the basic "wiring" of creation. It's built into everything around us, even if we can't immediately see it. Unfortunately, it's something that usually dawns on us only after we've tried everything else under the sun.

Being human, it often takes us some time in submitting to God and going through painful experiences to understand that this is the way things are. Let's get this truth straight as soon as possible so that we don't waste any more of our precious years learning it the hard way. Let's discover the good news in this passage that our personal fulfillment and well-being are on God's heart even before they're on ours, and he has the desire as well as the means to bring them about. We don't.

What do we lose if we give over our lives, aspirations, dreams, and hopes to God? In reality, nothing. Whatever we "lose" in this world for God, we receive many times over in return both in this present life and in the life to come (Mark 10:28–31).

So keep this in mind when you are praying for the things you want and need: if you do not receive what you ask for now, you've lost nothing, because in the end, you will have more than you ever dreamed. Yes, there is a cross of suffering and loss for the Christian in this life, but it's not even to be compared to the great glory and indescribable joy waiting for us.

TODAY'S PRAYER

Do you feel that in your life you've lost more than you've gained? Ask God for the assurance that in the life of faith nothing is ever really unrecoverable or in vain. He deliberately builds everything into his eternal purpose that far exceeds any of our hopes or expectations.

TODAY'S PROGRESS

_____

_____

_____

_____

_____

_____

_____

_____

Who's Behind It

For men are not cast off by the Lord forever. Though he
brings grief, he will show compassion, so great is his
unfailing love. For he does not willingly bring affliction
or grief to the children of men.

–LAMENTATIONS 3:31–33

This passage tells us that God is behind both the good and the bad we experience. Many think that God gives us the good, Satan gives us the evil, and that the two are warring with each other while we simply wait to see which one of them wins.

No, Satan the destroyer is surely and entirely evil and wants evil for us all the time and forever. But he can't do a single thing that God does not first permit. He's relatively free on this earth for a time, but he's always on a leash. He'll never be allowed to do all the evil he wants or to act as badly as he wants. God's power and goodness are far greater.

So there's always a huge gulf separating God from Satan, good from evil, but God can still bring us grief and affliction whenever it contributes in some way to our redemption or spiritual growth. It's due to our fallen state that this is even necessary. We simply don't pay much attention to God when things are sailing along nicely and we're healthy and prosperous. Sometimes God needs to give us a jolt to keep us from falling asleep at the wheel and going off the road. Sometimes he uses the bad times so we can be a witness to others, and sometimes in this life we just don't know all the reasons.

But what we can be sure of is that it's never his first desire to bring us affliction or distress, but he's more than willing to do so if it leads to our maturity or salvation. And that's the only reason it comes our way. Even if it comes as a form of judgment, it's still there with a motive of redemption. And there's the good news. We can remain positive and joyful even in the midst of affliction and suffering, whatever forms they take, because our welfare is behind them.

TODAY'S PRAYER

Do you think that bad things are happening to you because God is angry and is judging you for something? Pray that the Holy Spirit will enlighten your mind with the truth that, since he chose you for his own, whatever he permits to come your way is for your good.

TODAY'S PROGRESS

_____

_____

_____

_____

_____

_____

_____

_____

The Highest Appeal

He is the image of the invisible God, the firstborn over
all creation. For by him all things were created: things
in heaven and on earth, visible and invisible, whether
thrones or powers or rulers or authorities; all things
were created by him and for him. He is before all things,
and in him all things hold together.

–COLOSSIANS 1:15–17

When we pray in the name of Jesus, we are praying to the one described here. Jesus is the name above every name, the one who reigns over all other powers and authorities on the earth, spiritual or political. There is no person, employer, courtroom, judge, jury, president, or dictator who holds more power over you than the strong Son of God. He's the highest you can go when it comes to an appeal for help or justice. The apostle Paul says elsewhere:

> For God was pleased to have all his fullness dwell in him, and through him to reconcile to himself all things, whether things on earth or things in heaven, by making peace through his blood, shed on the cross. (Col. 1:19–20)

So there's no power available to us on earth that's greater than what Jesus holds in his hands. Nothing can happen to you or me that he's unaware of or that can confuse or surprise him. If it's happening, then it's happening by his permission, and it's something working for our good. It can't have any more authority over us than he allows, and there's no one who can have more power to deliver and rescue us than Jesus. That's something we can rest secure in.

As believers in Jesus, we have access to the highest court in the universe. Have you ever been so abused, mistreated, tricked, or defrauded that you wanted to present your whole case before some judge or jury? Have you ever longed for justice so much that it occupied your thinking every waking moment? If so, you're a candidate for the heavenly court that never adjourns. We can present all the facts before the King and the Prince of Heaven with the confidence that, at the right time (God's time) and in the right way (God's way), absolutely perfect justice will be done.

TODAY'S PRAYER

Lift up your complaint or request to God, the Judge of all things, by letting Jesus, your attorney, bring your case before God. Always keep in mind the high status of who Jesus is and the indescribable measure of his power and authority.

TODAY'S PROGRESS

_____

_____

_____

_____

_____

_____

_____

The Power of
Persistence

Then he said to them,

"Suppose one of you has a friend, and he goes to him at midnight and says, 'Friend, lend me three loaves of bread, because a friend of mine on a journey has come to me, and I have nothing to set before him.'

"Then the one inside answers, 'Don't bother me. The door is already locked, and my children are with me in bed. I can't get up and give you anything.' I tell you, though he will not get up and give him the bread because he is his friend, yet because of the man's boldness he will get up and give him as much as he needs.

"So I say to you: Ask and it will be given to you; seek and you will find; knock and the door will be opened to you. For everyone who asks receives; he who seeks finds; and to him who knocks, the door will be opened.

"Which of you fathers, if your son asks for a fish, will give him a snake instead? Or if he asks for an egg, will give him a scorpion? If you then, though you are evil, know how to give good gifts to your children, how much more will your Father in heaven give the Holy Spirit to those who ask him!"

–LUKE 11:5–13

A very important piece of the prayer puzzle is found in Jesus' teaching that persistence in prayer carries a lot of weight with God. He taught us to ask, seek, and knock. The grammar of this passage tells us something we need to know. The verb tense implies that we are to ask and keep on asking, seek and keep on seeking, knock and keep on knocking. In other words, we're not to give up easily but to press in on God and push our way forward into his presence.

No, this isn't being presumptuous or pushy. It's being persistent. And for reasons that he doesn't tell us, God likes it. Some commentators tell us that persistence changes us, not

God. The act of asking, seeking, and knocking over a long period of time transforms us. This is often the case, as the vast body of Christian biography tells us.

But Jesus doesn't explain exactly why we are to be persistent in prayer—he just tells us to pray this way. This may not appeal to our adult senses and reason, but it does appeal to a child. Children instinctively know how to ask and keep on asking almost to the point of going off the charts with persistence. It may be annoying to adults, but it often gets the job done for them. So let's start thinking like children (in this one respect). No, I don't mean develop a childish and silly theology, but come to God as his child in total dependence and confidence that what we say matters to him.

He wants us to bring our requests before him often. It may be just to clarify for us how important it is (or isn't). Haven't you ever stopped praying for something just because it didn't seem that important anymore or because you changed your mind? Thank God that he doesn't give us what we request within twenty-four hours!

So let's keep asking, seeking, and knocking. We are never to stop pressing our way into God's throne room because we think that he is tired of hearing us. Until he answers with a yes or a no, he wants us to keep moving forward, keep concentrating, and not give in or give up too soon. And sometimes a no simply means not yet.

The Little Things

Are not five sparrows sold for two pennies? Yet not
one of them is forgotten by God. Indeed, the very hairs
of your head are all numbered. Don't be afraid; you
are worth more than many sparrows.

–LUKE 12:6–7

This passage is packed with good news and reasons to live a forward-looking and positive life of thanksgiving and unflagging prayer. First of all, Jesus is affirming the high value of all his creatures. Do you like animals and birds? God likes them even more. He made them. Sparrows didn't count for much in the ancient world, but not one of them was ever outside the notice of their Creator.

So not only is every dog, cat, bird, mouse, giraffe, and elephant watched over and loved by God, but everything that's part of their lives is important to him. He isn't too busy to think of them. He feeds and provides for them, and we should watch out for their welfare too.

But as valuable to God as they all are, humans are even more valuable. Psalm 8 says we are the pinnacle of his creation. We occupy a special place in God's created order, and therefore we have a special vocation. With our high place in his eyes, we have not only high responsibilities but also high privileges.

Does God care about the minutiae of our personal lives? You bet he does. We tend to think that God is too big and too busy to bother himself with the very small, but he takes a deep interest in the thoughts, fears, questions, worries, and petty stuff that occupies most of our day—the tiny details unnotice-able to others. We often don't even want others to know what concerns us. It just seems too unimportant and irrelevant to talk or pray about.

But that's not the way it is with God. He's obviously aware of every thought we have and every motive behind every thought (1 Chron. 28:9b), so we might as well come clean with him and just tell him everything. Let God in on the little irrita-tions, the little problems, and even the little dreams that occupy our minds. He not only cares about them, he actually has the power to do something about them.

TODAY'S PRAYER

Ask the Creator of all things for a sweeping change in perspec-tive. Come to see everything (literally every last thing) in your life as having importance to God. Lift before him the very small as well as the very great.

TODAY'S PROGRESS

_____

_____

_____

_____

_____

_____

Hope, Now

How great is your goodness, which you have stored up for
those who fear you, which you bestow in the sight of men on
those who take refuge in you. In the shelter of your presence
you hide them from the intrigues of men; in your dwelling
you keep them safe from accusing tongues.

–PSALM 31:19–20

What's so encouraging about this and other passages like it is the hope of God's goodness and help, not just in the distant future beyond the present world but also in the here and now. We can trust God for his never-ending blessings after death, but we can also trust him for his help, rescue, protection, and defense from evil in what the psalmist calls "the land of the living" (Ps. 27:13).

King David was just as concerned as we are that God's blessings extend to the present, earthly life with all its disappointments, struggles, and sorrows. As with other Old Testament writers, he had a sense that this world was not all there is and that God has something in mind for us after we pass from the scene, but no one who lived before Jesus had any clear idea what that might look like.

Whereas the psalmist had a somewhat fuzzy idea of our future after this life but a sharper picture of God's present blessings, we, after the coming of Jesus, have a clear enough picture of the future but too often not a good idea of God's intent for us in the present. We tend to put off his best for the distant future because we think of our present history as a sort of second-rate reality to be discarded at the end for the real thing—heaven and the kingdom of God.

But this completely misreads the Bible. The future is important because it's built upon the present and the past. History (all history) is important because it is the launching pad of the ultimate future. It's all connected to God's great plan involving every bit of space and time from the creation of the world to his everlasting kingdom.

So we shouldn't be surprised to learn that God wants to extend his blessings and protection to us from birth to death, just as he has planned to carry us into his eternal blessing where no harm or evil can touch us ever again. Whatever he allows to happen to us now is always and forever for our good and will be used to prepare us for the unending joy he has stored up for us.

TODAY'S PRAYER

Are you tempted to think that you have to wait for the next life for God to bless you? Ask the Lord boldly for all your earthly needs. He loves to bless, protect, and vindicate his people.

TODAY'S PROGRESS

_____

_____

_____

_____

_____

In the Morning

*Weeping may remain for a night, but rejoicing comes in
the morning. . . . You turned my wailing into dancing; you
removed my sackcloth and clothed me with joy.*

–PSALM 30:5, 11

The psalmist is no stranger to weeping and mourning. The
theme appears often in the collection of psalms known as
the Psalter. We aren't strangers to pain and sorrow either. They
are a part of this life we live in, here and now, for each of us.

We can feel right at home with the words of David because
he's telling us not just about his feelings and what happened to
him, but also about what we can expect as well. Yes, like David
we'll inevitably suffer, but like David we'll see the morning
sunrise. We'll have our "sackcloth" removed and be clothed
with joy.

It's important to notice that the theme of joy in this present life is one that's generally lacking in the literature of the
ancient world. There wasn't too much to be joyful about in
the daily lives of most people (as is true of many today), yet in
both the Old and New Testaments it's striking that joy—even
great joy—is the mark of God's presence in the lives of human
beings. Where the Spirit of God is among his people, there is
the Spirit of joy and celebration.

Through King David's words, we are assured that suffering (whether it comes as a result of our own fault or someone
else's) is purely temporary. It's not permanent; it's not final; it's
not God's last word to us. So we can get through anything,

anything at all, if we know that it will pass away and only joy will remain.

TODAY'S PRAYER

Pray not only that God will meet the need that's upon your heart but also that he will grant his unique joy even in the period of waiting for him.

TODAY'S PROGRESS

Freedom

*The Spirit of the Lord is on me, because he has anointed me
to preach good news to the poor. He has sent me to proclaim
freedom for the prisoners and recovery of sight for the blind, to
release the oppressed, to proclaim the year of the Lord's favor.*

–LUKE 4:18–19

How many people think that Jesus came for the sole purpose
of bringing us into lives of mind-numbing boredom and
monastery-like religiosity?

For too many people, Jesus is a person who spends most
of his time in deep fear that somebody somewhere is having
a good time. How many people do you know who have some
interest in faith in Jesus but are putting it off for a while until
they get in all the fun and good times first?

But we can be glad that's way off the mark! Jesus came with
good news. He was sent to release people from every form of
captivity, blindness, and oppression. He was and is the bringer
of joy and celebration. Jesus brings the party with him. The
New Testament uses every possible image to show us that the
mission of Jesus in the world is joyful liberation. Pictures of huge
feasts, exaggerated joy, abundance—all of these are attempts to
tell us in the clearest possible language that God intends good
things for his creatures if they'll just pay attention to his guidance and receive his master plan over their own.

The entire Bible in all its complicated history is there
to communicate to us that God's will and purpose from the
beginning to this very day are to lead us away from despair and

death and into true and lasting life. If we hold to any view of the meaning of Jesus' gospel other than the fact that it's good news, then we can be sure that it's not the real gospel. Freedom for all who are trapped and imprisoned, restoration of sight for the blind, release from all sorts of oppression or depression, and proclamation of the Lord's favor—these are the details of the gospel Jesus brings to the world.

Let's keep this fixed in our minds and hearts as we continue to pray with confidence for an extravagant future.

TODAY'S PRAYER

When you are praying for your particular needs, go on and ask for the moon. Don't hold back. Pray for a full, many-sided liberation from all that oppresses and holds you back.

TODAY'S PROGRESS

_____

_____

_____

_____

_____

_____

_____

_____

As Far as the East Is from the West

Then I acknowledged my sin to you and did not cover up
my iniquity. I said, "I will confess my transgressions to the
LORD"—and you forgave the guilt of my sin.

–PSALM 32:5

Acknowledging our faults, weaknesses, and sins is not our idea of fun, and sometimes it's the last thing we ever want to do. So why is it so necessary to our spiritual health?

It's because without confession there is no forgiveness— and God's grace and forgiveness are the foundation of our relationship with him. If we are completely open with God about our sins, God is completely ready to forgive them. He wants to blot out our sins:

> For as high as the heavens are above the earth, so great is
> his love for those who fear him; as far as the east is from the
> west, so far has he removed our transgressions from us. (Ps.
> 103:11–12)

Think about it. The God who decrees that human sin deserves and receives death is the same God who also declares that he is more willing and ready to wipe it all out and bury it in the very depths of the sea than we are to admit it. He holds no grudges even though every bad thing we do or say is ultimately against him. He doesn't even remember our folly and foolishness if we allow him to dispose of it all in his giant refuse dump. It's gone. Done with. Forever!

There's really nothing in our earthly experience that prepares us for this level of forgiveness, grace, and mercy. People don't really forget, even though they may say they do. Given the right moment, we'll hear it all again: "Oh, you remember very well about that time you _____ [fill in the blank yourself]."

But with God, who has every right to remind us of our past failures, it's all gone and forgotten. He erases and blots out every last trace of the stain forever. Why? Just because that's the way he is. It's part of his unchangeable character.

TODAY'S PRAYER

Every time you lift up to God your needs and desires, don't forget to take advantage of your privilege of repentance. Keep the channels of communication unclogged with a free and clear conscience.

TODAY'S PROGRESS

_____

_____

_____

_____

_____

_____

Love

*A new command I give you: Love one another. As I have
loved you, so you must love one another.*

–JOHN 13:34

All the great commands of God are less of a "you must" and
more of a "you get to." Whenever God commands us to do
something, he's actually telling us how to live happy and fulfilled lives. Remember that when the Law of God was revealed
to his people, it was given expressly for their good (Deut. 10:13).

This is how we're supposed to look at all the command-
ments of God or Jesus. When Jesus gives his disciples a new
commandment, it's for their welfare, for them to live whole-
some and joyful lives, lives of deep meaning and great purpose.
He's given us in his ministry a model of what love is and how
it's supposed to be applied in life. He wants us to know that
if we'll live our lives in and with his love (and his help), we'll
be fulfilled in ways we couldn't even imagine. This kind of
love creates bonds that can't be broken even by death, bonds
that build and preserve friendships, families, communities, and
even nations.

When believers live intentionally by the kind of love Jesus
is talking about, a love that is a product of the Holy Spirit's
presence among us, it gains the attention of the world. People
aren't as interested in the doctrines we hold as in the way we live
and treat others, the way we care for them and give ourselves
for them. When they see something real here, they'll be more
interested in finding out what it is we believe.

And once we experience the new quality of Christ's unmistakable love, life takes on a new tang, a zest that will infuse us with the power to invade this present darkness. We carry the good news that this love is the central feature of God's purpose for human life. It's real. It's there for the taking. It's the only thing that can dispel the cynicism and grimness around us and truly make life worth living.

TODAY'S PRAYER

If you're wondering what your job description is in the period of waiting on God, then remember that love is Jesus' central command for the life of faith and one of the greatest joys you can ever experience.

TODAY'S PROGRESS

_____

_____

_____

_____

_____

_____

_____

_____

_____

Not Guilty

Therefore, there is now no condemnation for those who
are in Christ Jesus.

–ROMANS 8:1

Obviously, a lot has gone before this sentence, since it begins with the word "therefore." But it still stands by itself. It means what it says: In Jesus there is and can be no condemnation. All condemnation has taken place on the cross. It was entirely absorbed for us by his act of self-sacrifice. The death that was due to us because of our sin was taken upon Christ, in some way we can't fully comprehend, and we got off scot-free. It's as if we appeared before the Judge of the universe and heard, "Not guilty. Free to go."

That means no one else, no other power, not even our own conscience, has the right to condemn us. We are forgiven, our slate is clear, nothing stands against us, and we are free to enjoy the favor of God forever. It has nothing to do with how good or faithful we've been or how well we've performed. It has to do with how thoroughly God has dealt with our sins and failures and cast them into the depths of the sea to be buried forever.

This truth of God's forgiveness is something we need to bring to the forefront of our minds every day. It tends to fade as the pressures of the daily grind steadily displace the simple joy of first discovery. We should start every morning and end every evening with this comforting knowledge and quickly disregard every other counter-message from anyone around us (or even from an off-base or toxic church) that tries to penetrate our thinking.

Walk through each and every day with this confidence. There is no condemnation. If you fall, then get up, confess, and repent. The slate is clean again. God's mercies are fresh every morning. This is the foundation for optimistic living, one that is rooted not in us or our opinion of ourselves (good or bad) but in the unchanging character of God.

TODAY'S PRAYER

There's nothing that keeps us going through a long season of actively waiting prayer better than the confidence that we are free from condemnation and guilt. It's your inheritance. Enjoy it. Thank God for it.

TODAY'S PROGRESS

_____

_____

_____

_____

_____

_____

_____

_____

The Hiding Place

*You are my hiding place; you will protect me from trouble
and surround me with songs of deliverance.*

–PSALM 32:7

It was Corrie ten Boom who titled her amazing biography after this phrase in Psalm 32. In *The Hiding Place*, she tells of her experience in one of Hitler's worst concentration camps during World War II. We can't even imagine what it was like to go through the intensity of suffering there. But that was exactly where she learned firsthand what it meant to see God as a hiding place.

It wasn't that God hid her away from all the squalor and suffering of the death camp. It was that, in the midst of it, she was kept safe and whole as she found her safety in God's trustworthiness. She survived when so many others did not.

God grants these experiences not just for the growth of the one going through them, but for us as well. We profit from all the accounts of believers who have gone before us, for in a sense they form the archives of our family (our faith family) history. We have every right to claim all the true stories of believers throughout history (including biblical history) as our own. We need to know them, memorize the details, let them sink into our consciousness, and tell them to our children and grandchildren.

Let's never forget, God is our hiding place, our "fortress" (Ps. 46:7), who protects us from ultimate harm and often even from earthly sufferings and danger. He's the only truly reliable keeper and protector, the only absolutely trustworthy source of faithfulness and unwavering loyalty. So when everyone else around us is giving in to despair and fear, he is our foundation for remaining stubbornly positive.

TODAY'S PRAYER

As you pray today, remind yourself that you are safe in the hiding place God has created for you. Ask the Holy Spirit to make clear all the various advantages offered to you as you dwell securely in it.

TODAY'S PROGRESS

All of Creation

The creation itself will be liberated from its
bondage to decay and brought into the glorious
freedom of the children of God.

−ROMANS 8:21

If we jump on a train and don't know where it's going or what its destination is, we'll be confused and unsure about what to do. But thankfully, God gives us an unmistakably clear picture of what our final home will be.

That's what the apostle Paul is talking about here. What Isaiah called the new heaven and new earth, revisited in the Revelation of John (21:1–4) and alluded to in other parts of the New Testament, Paul describes as the liberation—the freeing from bondage—of all creation. Does he mean that we're all going to live in a state of disembodied souls in some cloud-like, gauzy heaven? Fortunately not! I don't know about you, but I don't look forward to spending eternity in the sky as a colorless gas. Rather he's using the language and imagery of the Old Testament in the light of the resurrection of Jesus to give us hope for the future.

Think about it this way: God has fixed a day on his calendar when he will speak the word of creation once again and recall into existence every person who loves his kingdom, and everything he ever created, to live forever on his new physical, full-color, immortal earth. All evil and evil people or spirits, all death and decay, all pollution, war, deceit, enmity, hatred, lust, greed, or anything else that dishonors God will be permanently removed, forever. Everything that is good about this world will be there, and everything bad will not.

So nothing but God's wonderful purpose and kingdom will exist. That's why we're encouraged to develop a taste for God's good will now, because there will come a time when we will enjoy nothing else but his grace and goodness toward us.

In the meantime, nothing we do in moving toward that goal will be a waste of time (1 Cor. 15:58). Absolutely nothing, either great or small—if it is in accordance with his will—will be in vain in preparing for the great conclusion of history. No prayer to God or effort for him will ever be a waste of time. With that in mind, let's keep focused in prayer and press forward to the goal, forgetting past regrets or negativity that try to keep us down. And let's do what's in front of us to do with faithfulness and integrity. It will all count in God's eyes.

TODAY'S PRAYER

As you pray for your temporal need today, keep your mind fixed on the end of the game. It's beyond even your best attempt to imagine it. It will keep you moving forward. It's real, and it's just ahead.

TODAY'S PROGRESS

_____

_____

_____

_____

_____

Always Reliable

*I was young and now I am old, yet I have never seen the
righteous forsaken or their children begging bread.*

–PSALM 37:25

The author of this psalm, King David, is just summarizing his own life experience of God. God proves himself reliable in real life!

David declared his solid trust in God because he'd never seen God forsake those who trusted him—however desperate the situation may have appeared at the moment—nor their children begging bread. He'd seen plenty of want and sorrow among those who trusted vainly in other gods and idols, but not among those who called on the Creator of the universe, the one true God, for help. This God will provide for our needs even when it seems impossible to us. There may be very lean days for us as well as periods of huge challenges (we're not promised a smooth sail), but as a general rule, our basic needs will be met.

Farther along in the psalm, David reiterates that "the salvation [rescue] of the righteous comes from the Lord; he is their stronghold in time of trouble" (verse 39). So we can be confident even in times of great want, because we have a wondrous God whose grace and mercy we can trust.

Yes, we'll always hear of someone somewhere in the world who doesn't have life's basic needs met. This is true even of believers who are suffering want, deprivation, imprisonment, and all the rest. We should be wary of "Christian advertising" suggesting that believers live within a protective bubble and will never suffer as others do. But at least four thousand years of Jewish and Christian history tell us we can be sure, even in those most severe cases, that God never abandons his people nor leaves them without hope or solace. If we wait patiently, we'll begin to hear those reports of divine help and mercy that the evening news forgot to cover.

TODAY'S PRAYER

As you bring your requests before God, remind him of his great faithfulness to those of old and of your confidence in him to meet every need in his time and way.

TODAY'S PROGRESS

_____

_____

_____

_____

_____

_____

_____

_____

_____

Worth the Wait

I waited patiently for the LORD; he turned to me and
heard my cry. He lifted me out of the slimy pit, out
of the mud and mire; he set my feet on a rock and
gave me a firm place to stand.

−PSALM 40:1−2

God is worth waiting for. In fact, he often makes us wait for him before he chooses to do anything for us. Why he does this is not always clear, but it is such a common experience among believers over the centuries that it seems more the rule than the exception. He wants us to wait, and to do so in patient trust that he will do something for us.

But this is exactly what we usually don't want. We want him to act for us—to heal, deliver, rescue, change circumstances, make a way out, lead us to a promised land, or whatever else—but we want it to happen right now, or next week at the latest. We're used to fast food and fast-acting detergent, instant messaging and instant gratification, so we don't look favorably upon a slow God.

Yet God often chooses to be slow. He's slow to anger and we're glad for that. He's not always quick to fix our problems for us because it's in the waiting that our faith grows—it stretches in that interim period between our prayer for deliverance and our rescue. And it's probably the norm for God to wait a good amount of time to do what we ask of him, because he likes to use time to do it. God created time (history), he likes time, and his plans require time to work out the way he wants. This is one of the leading themes of the Bible: God uses history as the main arena of salvation.

So we shouldn't be shocked, surprised, or discouraged when God takes his own time in working out his will for us. He may not be early (he won't be bullied or manipulated into acting before his plan takes shape), but he's never too late. And he'll work his will into our lives as we wait (patiently) for him. So stay positive in the waiting period, say and do positive things in the interim, because in time you won't be disappointed.

TODAY'S PRAYER

Are you beginning to think that nothing is ever going to change? That God isn't interested in your prayer? It's only an illusion. Don't give in to it. Keep presenting your needs with boldness and confidence. And thank God for the answer that's on the way.

TODAY'S PROGRESS

_____

_____

_____

_____

_____

_____

Real Life

But God demonstrates his own love for us in this: While we were still sinners, Christ died for us.

—ROMANS 5:8

Those of us raised in the Christian faith have heard this and similar passages so many times that it likely creates no real excitement in us. But try to imagine hearing this astonishing message for the first time: Long before we ever had the slightest interest in God, he had a very great interest in us. Years or decades before we came to conscious faith in Jesus, he was acting in and around us to draw us to him. His interest and action toward us always preceded ours toward him.

What this means is that we didn't and can't earn his favor or blessing or our salvation. It was bought and paid for in full on the cross where Jesus absorbed into himself all the penalty of our wrongdoing, bad decisions, rebellion, foolishness, and alienation from God. He didn't do it because we suddenly got so smart or came to our senses and decided to straighten out. No, he did it while we were happily skipping on our way toward destruction, oblivious to the cliff ahead and the rocks below. He blocked our way and rescued us. He then gave us a real life in both this world and the next just because he loves us so much and hates wasted human life.

This means salvation rests in God's hands, not ours. He started the whole thing in the first place and will bring it to completion. We don't know exactly why or how, only that it is in his heart to do it. So when we're tempted to think that we'll never make it on our own or that we'll never be holy enough or good enough to get there . . . we're right. We never will. We never can.

But we don't have to. That's the good news! Jesus outfits us for the journey. He finds us where we are (in our distrust, confusion, and wandering), equips us to get through this life (through our pain, losses, grief), then ushers us into God's kingdom at the end, fully prepared to meet our Creator. That's the gospel. There is nothing in this world better than that.

Listen to the great summary of the gospel from the end of the letter of Jude:

> To him who is able to keep you from falling and to present you before his glorious presence without fault and with great joy—to the only God our Savior be glory, majesty, power and authority, through Jesus Christ our Lord, before all ages, now and forevermore! Amen. (Jude 1:24–25)

TODAY'S PRAYER

Never give in to the voice that whispers over your shoulder while you're praying, "Give up: you're wasting your time. God doesn't listen to sinners like you." Instead, be even bolder in setting your need before God and thanking him for his great love.

TODAY'S PROGRESS

_____

_____

_____

_____

Don't Be Afraid

*For I am the L*ORD*, your God, who takes hold of your right*
hand and says to you, Do not fear; I will help you.

−ISAIAH 41:13

What is it that most effectively causes a child to lose fear? Is it our lecture on the nature of fear, or our telling them there's no reason to be afraid? Or is it because we take the child by the hand and say, "Don't be afraid, I'm with you"? All the child really needs to know is whether the loving parent or guardian is going to be by his or her side.

It's pretty much the same with us. Every verbal encouragement in the world will have little impact compared to the assurance that God knows our situation and promises to take us by the hand and lead us through it. Just hearing "Don't be afraid" is very much like hearing "Don't get lost" or "Don't get sick." It's all just worthless advice unless there's some power, help, or guidance available to us.

The sole grounds for our fearlessness is nothing but the powerful presence of God. He imparts his own fearlessness to us only as we are in relationship to him. If we want nothing to do with his presence or help, then we'll never know what it's like to walk through the valleys hand in hand with our Creator instead of frightened and alone.

If we try to fix things on our own or move ahead under our own steam, we discover that the wind is just too strong and the way is too steep for us. It's typical of us humans to underestimate the power of the storm and overestimate our own resources in getting through it. One of the chief lessons we learn in life is that we are not the stand-alone pillars of strength we thought we were and that we desperately need a helper who is willing to take us by the hand and guarantee us the strength we need to get through every trial. So let's continue to pray and confidently walk forward with our hand firmly in his.

TODAY'S PRAYER

Don't be hesitant to say to God today, "I'm afraid. Draw me closer to you."

TODAY'S PROGRESS

_____

_____

_____

_____

_____

_____

_____

_____

_____

_____

The Destination

I consider that our present sufferings are not worth comparing with the glory that will be revealed in us.

−ROMANS 8:18

Have you ever heard the Navy Seal motto during "Hell Week" (the last week of training)? It goes like this: "Pain is good. Extreme pain is extremely good." Well, maybe that doesn't ring true to you, particularly if you're in pain right now. But if you get the point, it really does make good sense. The pain of training is not to be compared with the glory and satisfaction of being declared part of the elite Navy Seals. The end product is worth the high price.

Paul wants us to know that our present sufferings (and he had plenty of his own) are nothing compared to the joy that is to come. The great glory, majesty, and just plain joy of being part of God's final wrap-up of history will cause every present pain and loss to fade into oblivion—forever. It won't even be a memory there.

We can get through anything if the destination is far better than the ride. In this life, we'll all get our share of suffering—no one really escapes. Some will have more and some less, but each of us will face the wall. Yet as followers of Jesus, we should keep in mind that the "end" (not just the *termination* but the *destination*) will be so far off the charts that our scars in getting there, as great as they may seem, will be so slight that they won't even be worth mentioning.

We tend to say things like, "When I get there, I've got a

lot of questions for God about this!" But when we do get there, the indescribable glory of what will lie before us will make any such questions too irrelevant and silly even to think about. If we keep our mind focused on that truth, we can get through whatever struggle we face today.

TODAY'S PRAYER

If the strain of the day blurs the destination for you, then ask God to enliven and make clear the joy and glory both of the final end and of the pure pleasure of his deliverance on this side.

TODAY'S PROGRESS

_____

_____

_____

_____

_____

_____

_____

_____

_____

_____

Stress-free

Cast your cares on the LORD and he will sustain you; he
will never let the righteous fall.

—PSALM 55:22

You've probably noticed that anxiety and distress can make you sick, while joy can actually heal you. No one ever got sick and died because of too much happiness or a too-carefree life! This fact, now more and more a part of research in the wellness and healing arts, gives us a clue about our original design.

The secret is this: we're hardwired for joy and stress-free living. God created us to live lives of simple trust in him and to thrive when we are as free from distress and anxiety as possible. Jesus taught this same thing when he gave instructions on how to be his follower (Matt. 6:25–34). Peter reiterated the words of Psalm 55 and of Jesus when he encouraged his readers: "Cast all your anxiety on him because he cares for you" (1 Peter 5:7).

All this means that we are not to carry around with us all the burdens and worries that weigh us down every day. We're not supposed to because we're not designed even to try. Anxiety and stress are a total and complete waste of time and energy. They don't do us the slightest bit of good and, in the long run, can do a great deal of damage.

So dump it, toss it off, get rid of it as soon as possible! Cast it off your shoulders, and let God do the caring and the carrying for you. Everything's in his hands anyway. Of course, it's not easy to do. God knows that too. But it can be done in the same way that any of his commands can be done. The church father Augustine prayed: "Lord, give what you command." God knows that we can't keep his will perfectly, but he has made provision to help us keep it.

The key lies in the constant reminder that we aren't able, but God is; and in the daily discipline of turning over to him all our anxieties, we begin to change from the worrywarts we are and gradually move into a life of lighthearted obedience. It's time and experience that count here. That's why God uses time (and lots of it) to get his will done in us.

So stay positive. Think, speak, and act day by day knowing that he is accomplishing his work in us. One day, with God's help, you and worry will part ways.

TODAY'S PRAYER

Do you find yourself continually returning to the worry that Jesus forbids? This is the norm for fallen human beings everywhere, so ask the Holy Spirit repeatedly to take it from you. Confess that you can't do it, but he can.

TODAY'S PROGRESS

_____

_____

_____

_____

_____

_____

Vision of the Air

And we know that in all things God works for the
good of those who love him, who have been called
according to his purpose.

—ROMANS 8:28

There is an incredible amount of good news packed into this one verse. In this letter, Paul is saying that everything in life that happens to us (everything!) is the raw material God decides to use to bring us (and others) something good. No, it doesn't mean that God smiles benignly upon all the evil that happens in this world or that he has no standards of right and wrong or that he never judges and punishes the bad. It means that, by his own power and wisdom, he brings good out of the bad to suit his purposes.

In World War I, when a fighter pilot first went into the air, he hadn't yet acquired the skill to see everything going on around him. As he gained more experience, he started to see the details that had escaped him earlier—enemy fighter planes over, around, and above him. This maturity was referred to as the "vision of the air."

Similarly we have what may be called "eyes of faith"—faith that matures and moves from something that may be fairly tentative and unsure, to a matter of genuine confidence and security. It graduates from "I hope so" to "I know so." What we learn is that God uses the bad that happens to us (all of it, every last trace) to bring into our lives the good he wants for us, whatever anyone else's intentions are. Others may set out to harm us, but God turns it for our good (check out Genesis 50:20, our Day 3). Only he can do that. We can't.

So the good that God intends to bring us is not *in spite of* but *because of* the bad that occurs. God has a way of entering into and transforming situations so that their end is surprisingly out of line with anything expected. He transforms things into what he wants and we need.

When we realize this, it will change the way we see everything. If we understand that God really does get involved in everything that affects us, that he's our overseer and friend who holds all power in his hands and controls everything that happens, then we can move forward knowing there isn't anything to fear—nothing can truly harm us—and failure or disaster can never really destroy us.

TODAY'S PRAYER

God doesn't expect us to thank him for the evil that comes our way, but he wants us to thank him today that he is now using that evil to bring good our way.

TODAY'S PROGRESS

_____

_____

_____

_____

_____

_____

No Fear

*The L*ORD *is my light and my salvation—whom shall I*
*fear? The L*ORD *is the stronghold of my life—of whom*
shall I be afraid?

−PSALM 27:1

Why does the Bible speak so often about fear? It's probably because fear is constantly around us and we're always fighting it. And the reason we face fear so often is because we chronically lapse into the same stubborn self-reliance that got history's first humans into trouble. It's our nature (our fallen nature) to go about our daily business thinking we are in charge of our own lives and everything is up to us, to depend on our own wisdom, strength, and skills more than on God's faithfulness and power. But it becomes clear that this definitely isn't the case whenever we face fear—something that's out of our control and that we can't handle by ourselves.

King David was no stranger to fear. We tend to think that the heroes of the Bible were all extraordinary people who never had to face all the same frailties we do. But the truth is just the opposite. They were just like the rest of us!

Three of the major heroes of the Bible were guilty of some of the worst sins and crimes—Moses was a murderer, David was a murderer and an adulterer, and Paul was a slayer of Christians. The Bible doesn't deal only with the saintly, good, and righteous. No, it deals with everyday people—sinners, failures, criminals, hypocrites, weaklings, cowards, and all the rest.

That's good news for us. It means that mercy and salvation

are for us, too, that all God's gifts are offered to the worst of us as well as the best. God wants to be our light and salvation—our light through the darkness, our guide through the wilderness, and our salvation in this life and the next. And if we know that God is right by our side through everything we experience, guiding us into a future he has already seen, we really have nothing to fear.

TODAY'S PRAYER

Pray that God will make his strength and power as real and near today as the psalmist came to see. Let God remind you that fear is simply unrealistic.

TODAY'S PROGRESS

_____

_____

_____

_____

_____

_____

_____

_____

Live Forever

Everyone who calls on the name of the Lord will be saved.

—ROMANS 10:13

This and other simple, straightforward statements end the debate on who will and can be saved for eternal life. Each of the world's religions has its own version of what salvation is and who can reach it, but Jesus offers the only form of eternal existence really worth talking about: a real physical life on a real physical planet, one that's been thoroughly purified of any evil or suffering and that's in every way more than and higher than this present life.

Who qualifies for this eternal kingdom of joy? Is it whoever does the best in life or works the hardest or is the most sincere and accomplishes the greatest things spiritually? According to the major religions of the world, salvation is something to be achieved, a reward given to those who qualify, normally by self-effort—keeping the rules, being part of the right group, following the rites, and generally fulfilling the requirements.

But this is far from what the gospel of Jesus declares. On the contrary, the saved are those who call on the name of the Lord. In other words, the person who spends eternity in the presence of the Creator, in the kingdom designed for his creatures, is simply the person who wants to be there. It's the criminal on the cross, the prostitute on the street, the miserable addict, and everyone else who realizes that they can't do a single thing to earn salvation or be good enough to make it on their own.

All that's really expected of us to gain eternity is to want it enough to drop all our prideful pretensions and ask for it, to call on the Lord's name in surrender and gratitude, to receive this wonderful present freely and joyfully, like a child at Christmas. What guarantees our membership in the kingdom of God is God's mercy and love of granting his gifts to his creatures. Thankfully it's not up to us. And since it's not up to us, we can be sure we're safe.

TODAY'S PRAYER

Don't let the thought creep into your mind that you haven't been good enough lately for God to hear your prayers. Always remember that the same grace that saved you is the same basis on which he answers you.

TODAY'S PROGRESS

_____

_____

_____

_____

_____

_____

_____

_____

In Control of the Sea

God is our refuge and strength, an ever-present help in trouble.
Therefore we will not fear, though the earth give way and the
mountains fall into the heart of the sea, though its waters roar
and foam and the mountains quake with their surging.

—PSALM 46:1–3

The Hebrews had a great respect and fear of the sea because for them it was the symbol of evil and chaos. There were all sorts of things in it that could hurt them. That's why the apostle John was shown a vision of the future, unshakable kingdom where there was no more sea (Rev. 21:1), a way of saying that evil and chaos wouldn't be there. But in the meantime, chaos and evil seem at times to run rampant with no boundaries on what they can do.

Evil is always on a leash and can do no more than God allows, but sometimes that's just not evident. Evil surges like the sea and great waves can arise from nowhere to carry us away with their power. Yet the psalmist, who knew plenty about life's troubles, was absolutely convinced that God is in total control of all things at all times and remains for us a refuge and strength. He was and is an ever-present help in time of trouble.

No matter what kind of belief system someone might have, when you're totally alone, floating on a life raft at sea surrounded by man-eating sharks, you need more than a belief system! You need someone powerful enough to come and rescue you.

Our prayers need to reflect this confidence. There isn't the slightest reason to doubt God's faithfulness toward us, and there is every reason to cling to it. If God hasn't acted on our behalf yet, it's merely a matter of our imperfect perception of things. He is ever-present whether we see him or not, and he is our help in times of trouble whether he chooses to relieve our distress now or later. In either case, it's all according to his purpose and what he is accomplishing by the difficulties of the moment.

We tend to have short memories in these matters and quickly forget those times when God delivered us. Today's crisis trumps yesterday's rescue. But God isn't as fickle as we usually are toward him, and he doesn't change his mind about us overnight. So keep yesterday clearly in mind because our history shapes the way we see our future.

TODAY'S PRAYER

Are you getting weary today of waiting and praying? It might be time for some remembrance. Keep your history before you by recalling all that God has done for you and all his people. He was never too early or too late. Now thank him for his faithfulness that never changes.

TODAY'S PROGRESS

_____

_____

_____

_____

_____

The Gift of Suffering

For it has been granted to you on behalf of Christ not
only to believe on him, but also to suffer for him, since
you are going through the same struggle you saw I had,
and now hear that I still have.

−PHILIPPIANS 1:29−30

What Paul is saying in this passage can easily slip by us in a too-quick reading. Suffering has been *granted* to us. It has been given or assigned to us just as it has been given or assigned to us to believe. (That's right, even our faith has been granted to us). This goes against our grain because it just doesn't seem right to us that God would actually bring suffering our way, particularly if we've been raised with the view that expects only prosperous and happy times to come from God's hand.

But the suffering referred to is what has been granted on behalf of Christ, our Lord. Jesus himself promised his followers that just as he was persecuted and abused and suffered in this life, so they shouldn't expect anything easier. As for the Master, so for us his servants. It can't be any other way. Paul is saying, "It happened to Jesus, you saw it happening to me, too, and now it's happening to you."

So we shouldn't be surprised at any sufferings that come our way. There are no free passes in the Christian life. We live in a world that doesn't recognize Jesus as Lord of all history and life; we live in a world with hostile forces or demonic powers all around us. That's all a given. The solution is not to imagine that life is other than what it is, but to understand and rejoice that in the midst of our troubles and persecutions stands the God who never abandons nor forsakes us.

What we really need to keep in mind at all times is that the suffering we go through has a purpose. It's not random or meaningless. It comes with an assignment of its own—to mature us, make us stronger, and enable us to bear witness to the world that there is a strength and a comfort available to suffering people who will reach out and receive it. That's the message a broken and wounded world needs to hear. And if they don't hear it from us, where else will they hear it?

TODAY'S PRAYER

Ask God to forgive all the very human whining and complaining and to grant you a vision for the final product of your suffering—a mature, confident, joyful, and useful servant of his kingdom.

TODAY'S PROGRESS

_____

_____

_____

_____

_____

_____

_____

Things We Can't Fix

Call upon me in the day of trouble; I will deliver you,
and you will honor me.

–PSALM 50:15

This is one of those great passages we learn in Sunday school and pack away until one day it comes to mind long after we've forgotten God and gone our own way. It pops into our head when we find ourselves in some sort of distress that we can't fix. Fortunately for us, God doesn't say, "Well, you managed to do without me all those years, so don't bother crawling back to me now when you're in trouble!" He's not spiteful or resentful. He really does want us to call upon him, even if we've never done so before or if we are doing so now only because we've tried everything else and nothing worked.

God has rescued and delivered people from literally every sort of evil or human impossibility. But the real test comes when we do call on him in trouble, expect his rescue, and trust that he'll come to our aid as promised, but he seemingly doesn't. He appears to be just sitting idly on the sidelines watching and not lifting a finger to help.

Does this describe your situation?

If so, there are a few things to remember. It's God who defines the extent of the promise to deliver in times of trouble, not us. We aren't the ones to decide just how and when he's going to step in and make things better. If so, God wouldn't be God; he would be a genie in a bottle. God knows how to rescue, but he also knows when *not* to rescue if a too-quick deliverance would run against his purpose. There is something important he wants to accomplish by bringing difficulties into our lives. And until that's accomplished, he'll allow the trouble to continue.

Of course, this isn't always pleasing to hear. We want things taken care of right now. We have people to see and places to go, and we don't have time to spend dealing with inconveniences. But God does. He has more time than we do, so it won't do any good trying to outpace him. We have every right to expect him to come and help in times of trouble, but we can't prescribe the when and how. That's for him to decide, and it's all based on a purpose that overarches our lives and far exceeds our own puny plans. He won't compromise his plan in order to accommodate ours, simply because his is infinitely better for us.

TODAY'S PRAYER

Remember, if it takes one hundred days or two hundred days, God will never modify his schedule in order to win our vote. Pray for his strength to go the distance and, in doing so, to win the prize of his deliverance.

TODAY'S PROGRESS

_____

_____

_____

_____

_____

_____

DAY 47

When Heaven
Meets Earth

The kingdom of heaven is near.

—MATTHEW 10:7B

This sounds good and seems simple enough. But what does it mean?

Ordinarily we tend to think that heaven is a place so far away that it goes beyond the farthest reaches of our universe. It's where God, Jesus, the angels, and our long-departed grandparents live. It's where most Christians believe they'll be someday.

But this is wide of the mark. The situation is really much better and more beneficial for us. Heaven is the realm of God, that part of the universe where he dwells in pure spirit. But it's not light years away—it's right next door. In fact, it's just about three inches above our heads. Remember the way we thought about it in Day 19: Separating heaven and us is a sort of very porous membrane through which all kinds of things can and do pass. If we had eyes to see (as Jesus did), we could witness the very heavy traffic between the two.

God breaks through to act on our behalf. Jesus moves back and forth between the Father's presence and ours millions of times a day, rescuing, healing, speaking, guiding. God can hear even a whisper when we're too tired or weak to pray, because he's so near. Someday heaven will "descend" (but not far) upon our earth to meet it and transform it into heaven's likeness:

Then I saw a new heaven and a new earth, for the first heaven and the first earth had passed away, and there was no longer any sea. I saw the Holy City, the new Jerusalem, coming down out of heaven from God, prepared as a bride beautifully dressed for her husband. And I heard a loud voice from the throne saying, "Now the dwelling of God is with men, and he will live with them. They will be his people, and God himself will be with them and be their God." (Rev. 21:1–3)

Jesus expects us to take his teaching seriously, so seriously that we revise our understanding of the world and the universe. He wants us to view the cosmos with new eyes—to grasp that our Creator is so near, as close as the parent is to the child, that all of life is to be lived under his watchful eye.

If we can get this right, if we can live this way, we'll find that life will take on a new meaning where pessimism and negative thinking are wholly out of touch with reality.

TODAY'S PRAYER

Ask God for new, unclouded lenses to see clearly what's really there. Pray that you can live a life in the fast lane where all the host of heaven is moving with you in the same direction.

TODAY'S PROGRESS

_____

_____

_____

_____

_____

How Long, O Lord?
And Other Stories

*Do you not know? Have you not heard? The LORD
is the everlasting God, the Creator of the ends of
the earth. He will not grow tired or weary, and his
understanding no one can fathom.*

–ISAIAH 40:28

Complaining about God is not some new innovation known only to our generation. People were complaining about him long before any of us ever got here. The ancient Hebrews were specialists in it and fine-tuned it into an art form.

"Where is God?" "Why has he forgotten me?" "How long, O Lord?" "Why doesn't he hear me?" And on and on. Sound familiar? Then know that you're in good company. Some of the greatest saints in history have far outdone you in the art of complaining. It's just part of our makeup, or at least our fallen nature. We often think that God exists mainly for our benefit and pleasure.

So we need frequent reminders that he's God and we aren't. Not that most of us sit around thinking we're the Creator of the universe, it's just that we find ourselves drifting into the belief that we are the center of it. We need to hear once again that the Lord is the everlasting God, the Creator of the earth. He deserves all glory, honor, love, worship, and service. But at the same time, we need to be reminded that he won't grow tired or weary, and his understanding no one can fathom.

All this is in our favor. It's true that he doesn't exist for our pleasure—we exist for his. But he is always there for us and wants our highest good even more than we do. He'll never get tired or weary in carrying out his plan for his universe (and his people). So if God weren't on our side, we'd be in deep trouble. What great news it is that he's stubbornly "us-ward" in all that he does and that he aims his inexhaustible energy and wisdom in our direction! We can bank on all this as we continue our prayer.

TODAY'S PRAYER

It's okay to ask God to forgive your complaints. Pray that he will bring to you a new understanding of his plan so that you will come to appreciate his ways (and timing) in carrying out his will for you.

TODAY'S PROGRESS

_____

_____

_____

_____

_____

_____

_____

_____

"I Chose You"

*You did not choose me, but I chose you and appointed you
to go and bear fruit—fruit that will last. Then the Father
will give you whatever you ask in my name.*

—JOHN 15:16

In the church today, we talk a lot about "making Jesus Lord"
or choosing Jesus or making a decision for him. But Jesus
spoke more often of his choosing us, appointing us, calling us
out from the crowds. In other words, it is Jesus, not we, who
plays the central role in God's program. In fact, we're taught
that unless Jesus gives his personal permission, we can't even
choose him in the first place (Matt. 11:27; Luke 10:22).

Many don't like this point and try hard to find ways around
it, but it's still true. Both Testaments confirm the same thing.
It's God who first calls us, who first moves upon us, implants
in us the desire for him, and then draws us toward himself by
arranging the right circumstances, often in spite of ourselves.

What this means for us is that we're safe. We're secure in
his care because he's the Author of our salvation and we aren't.
It's due to the Father's choosing power that we'll live fruitful
lives and that our lives will therefore be brought in line with
his will so we can receive his blessings as we ask for them.
Incidentally, this is really what it means to pray in Jesus'
name. "This is the confidence we have in approaching God: that if we
ask anything according to his will, he hears us" (1 John 5:14).

If we imagine that everything is up to us, we won't be able
to sustain a hopeful view of life for very long because it doesn't

take long to see that our own efforts are pretty ineffectual. Even our faith (what we usually congratulate ourselves for) is in reality a gift from God. He chooses to give it to us, and when we seem to lose it, he gives it back again. If we know that ultimately our lives are in God's hands, that we are his choice, then we'll find our hope-filled outlook in his predictably merciful and gracious character.

TODAY'S PRAYER

Here's one more reason to thank God for today. All his choices for us, whether pleasant for the moment or not, are for our good and were in his mind before the foundation of the world.

TODAY'S PROGRESS

_____

_____

_____

_____

_____

_____

_____

_____

_____

_____

Ask for the Impossible

"I am the LORD, the God of all mankind. Is
anything too hard for me?"

–JEREMIAH 32:27

Although the original context of God's question was God's
promise to bring his people into captivity because of
their disobedience, nevertheless it applies to any and all circumstances. The question is all-inclusive: Is there anything,
anything at all, that God can't do? And of course the answer is:
absolutely nothing.

There are other places in the Bible where the same issue
comes up, either in the form of a question or simply a statement.
Sometimes in our pride or blindness we think we're riding too
high to be brought down, and other times that things are so low
already that they're beyond all hope. In both cases the answer
is the same: God is in a position to do whatever he wants at any
time, under any circumstance.

The words "too hard" and "God" just don't go together.
Do you think the situation you face today is simply too far
advanced to fix or that there are no conceivable solutions open
to you? That's just the sort of problem God likes to take on.
It's his favorite thing to do. When every human resource is
exhausted and every brilliant idea fails to work, that is the very
moment for God to step in and take over.

But still we are taught to ask. He usually doesn't step in and
fix things if we want him to stay away. If we don't ask, how else
will we know that he answers our prayers? Think about it: God

always knows when he's doing something for us, but we know only if we ask.

Some people just never reach the point where they think their abilities and intelligence need assistance—"God helps those who help themselves" or "I don't need any God." That kind of thing. These are the people who never really understand that God grants us every day of our life.

So asking God to do the very hard or the utterly impossible is simply acknowledging that what we usually take as automatic is God's deliberate gift to us all along. Thinking that it's normally due to our own cleverness is self-delusion anyway. Prayer is a continual petition to grant what is beyond us and too impossible to do on our own, the very great and the very small. What we are doing in this 100-day period is daily lifting up to God all those things that come only from his generous hand. Nothing is the slightest bit more difficult for him to do than anything else. So while we're asking, why not ask for the moon?

TODAY'S PRAYER

Feel just as free to ask God for the utterly impossible as you do for anything else that seems merely difficult. In his eyes, it's all the same. He can create the solution or open a door where none existed before.

TODAY'S PROGRESS

_____

_____

_____

_____

The Silent
Heaven

Have you ever prayed and prayed day and night and felt as though God just wasn't listening? If so, you're not alone. Listen to King David's complaint:

> *My God, my God, why have you forsaken me?*
> *Why are you so far from saving me,*
> *so far from the words of my groaning?*
> *O my God, I cry out by day, but you do not answer,*
> *by night, and am not silent. (Ps. 22:1–2)*

This has been the complaint of believers for generations. But with each new generation, we learn a few things about what our prayer life involves. Let's start with Jesus' life.

In John 5:16–20, we find in metaphorical language what amounts to a parable of the carpenter's apprentice. Jesus says, "I tell you the truth, the Son can do nothing by himself; he can do only what he sees his Father doing, because whatever the Father does the Son also does" (v. 19). The imagery is that of a master craftsman and his trainee, reflecting Jesus' early learning as a carpenter. He tells us that his power in ministry didn't come from his natural identity as the strong Son of God, Co-Creator of the universe, and second member of the Trinity, but rather from his daily dependence on God in prayer.

In other words, he didn't take advantage of any power that wasn't available to us. He could have, but he didn't, because he wanted to live a human—not a superhuman—life. His power came from his "abiding place" in the Father, the same quality of life available to us by his sacrificial death on the cross.

In John 14, Jesus states that his followers will do amazingly great things in his name. When our prayers aren't answered, we tend to discard this promise. But praying "in Jesus' name" doesn't mean just saying "in Jesus' name" (like Ali Baba saying "Open Sesame" in just the right tones) and every wish is granted. It means praying in his great purpose and by the same power. In other words, we have to be involved in his will for our prayers to make a difference. If heaven seems silent and God doesn't seem to be responding to our prayers, then we need to find out if our plans and purposes are aligned with his perfect will for our lives.

In Luke 22:42, we discover the secret of Jesus' prayer life. He ended his prayers with the qualifier, "Not my will but yours be done." He lived out his entire earthly life with the acknowledgment of the higher order of things. He was trying to teach us something we need to know. The Father has a plan and purpose far higher than ours, but the happy result of this is that his plan is us-ward. It's designed to be on our side and for our good.

God may appear to us as silent or unresponsive to our most fervent prayers, but often it's just that he takes his time in answering. When we pray, we want an answer no later than tomorrow. But it may be in his plan to answer a week from tomorrow or a month from tomorrow or a year from tomorrow. Sometimes it's because the purposes of others' lives are tied up in this one answer. Whenever the answer comes, it will be on time.

And always remember: God's no may be only a not yet. If it's a permanent no, then it's for our good. If it's a not yet, it means that his plan is in progress.

Beyond Random

From one man he made every nation of men, that they
should inhabit the whole earth; and he determined the times
set for them and the exact places where they should live.

−ACTS 17:26

Don't you ever wonder why you live where you do, in the years you do, with the friends you have, and within your own language and culture? Why weren't you born in 1620? Or 1054? Or 432 BC? Maybe you would prefer to live in some other century or in some other country. But what this statement from the apostle Paul means is that you and I are here where we are and in the times we live by divine assignment.

We are given our families, years of birth and death, nations, languages, experiences, and all the rest because God put us where we are. He laid it all out on the drawing board and is every day carrying out his plan right on time and in all the right places. Every human being who has ever lived, regardless of his or her circumstances, has been assigned the time and place for a purpose. We can ignore that purpose and waste our entire lives in selfish and foolish pursuits, but that doesn't negate the fact that we were first put here for great and glorious ends.

God expects us to search out and find what our purpose is, and he makes it fairly simple to find if we're really looking for it. If most never do find it, it's not because the answers aren't there. But just think about it! Life is divinely appointed. It comes with the stamp of God upon it. It's to be lived according to his rules and his master plan.

When we live like this, our life makes sense, leads some-where, has both a purpose and a destination, and is heavily loaded with meaning. Everything that happens, both good and bad, from the moment of birth to the last breath, is governed by the infinite intelligence and mercy of our Creator. There's not an ounce of chance or randomness in God's arrangements for us.

TODAY'S PRAYER

Thank God for his plan for all the boundaries of your life and ask him to sharpen your understanding of his very specific purpose for you.

TODAY'S PROGRESS

_____

_____

_____

_____

_____

_____

_____

_____

_____

Anger and Patience

The LORD is gracious and compassionate, slow to anger and rich in love. The LORD is good to all; he has compassion on all he has made.

—PSALM 145:8-9

What a relief! God could have been anything he wanted to be, but he is actually gracious and compassionate. In our Western or "Christianized" world, we're so used to hearing about "amazing grace" that it doesn't seem so amazing anymore. Most of us are just plain spoiled. We have very little idea of what it means to live under a curse rather than a blessing. So we assume that if there is a God, he must be merciful and gracious, and if he's not living up to our perception of him, then he is cruel and unjust.

We often ask, "How can God allow all this evil in the world? How can God allow this to happen to me?" Many of the ancient Greeks and Romans would never have framed the questions that way because they saw their gods as capricious and uncaring, or even cruel. We ask such questions because we begin with the belief that the one true God is good, just, and righteous at all times. We can enjoy personal security and be hopeful when those around us are coming apart because God is slow to anger and rich in love.

Yet how many times do we wish he weren't quite so slow to anger when it comes to some people? We like and want for ourselves a God slow to anger but one quick to condemn our enemies. But he's the same for us as for those we very much want punished, and it's in this generous characteristic of our Father that we find our safety. The same feature of God that makes him slow to anger against people we don't like is what works in our favor as well.

So don't worry that your enemies haven't been utterly defeated. Instead, rejoice in God's patience and be glad that he has compassion for all he has made. Whatever pain we may be going through right now, he's nearer than we might think. He understands how we feel, even the things we can't express or that no one else ever knows. He feels for us in ways we can't even imagine, and he always cares enough to pick us up where we are and to carry us to that place of hope and joy he tailor-makes just for us.

TODAY'S PRAYER

Begin by thanking God for his extravagant mercy and patience toward you. Then ask him to bring to mind all the people who have offended or hurt you and are in need of your mercy and patience. Make this your prayer project for the day.

TODAY'S PROGRESS

_____

_____

_____

_____

_____

_____

The Plan

"For I know the plans I have for you," declares the LORD,
"plans to prosper you and not to harm you, plans to give
you hope and a future. Then you will call upon me and
come and pray to me, and I will listen to you. You will seek
me and find me when you seek me with all your heart."

—JEREMIAH 29:11–13

As with so many of the wonderful Old Testament promises to be fulfilled in the future, this one comes not because God's people were so good, but in spite of the fact that they were so bad. If God's blessings and favor were based upon how excellently we've behaved, then we're all in big trouble! Thankfully God doesn't work that way.

Israel was in exile when this word came to them. God permitted them to be taken captive by a foreign power because of their consistent, stubborn rebellion against his good purpose for them. They just knew better than God. Doing what the first humans did in the garden of Eden, they wanted to determine for themselves what was right and good, what was true for them. Things like truth and justice or the divine purpose meant nothing to them. So to preserve them from destruction as a people, God put them through a time of discipline and correction.

All along, God had a plan for them. He called them back to that plan when the time was right and reminded them that his purpose was always to prosper them and not to harm them, to give them hope and a future. In fact, what God wanted for people from the very beginning was for them to thrive, to prosper, to live fully and joyfully in the paradise he had created for them. But humanity has chosen ever since to live in the squalor and confinement of self-will and selfishness.

Even so, his promise still stands. He continues to renew his original plan generation after generation. It's there for us today, at this very moment. He can break our shackles forged by our sin and foolish choices and set us free to pursue the way that leads to everlasting life. And the best part is that this quality of life begins here and now. God's blessing and prosperity extend not only through this earthly life but also into the world to come. There's no downside. It's all good.

There's only one qualification: he wants us to seek him with all our heart. When he becomes number one in our lives, when and only when we acknowledge him as God and king, our life will straighten out, be turned right-side-up, and become what it was designed to be.

TODAY'S PRAYER

Ask the Holy Spirit to reveal to you any hidden areas of your life that are roadblocks to his blessings for you. Ask him for his supernatural power to hold him first in your life above all else.

TODAY'S PROGRESS

_____

_____

_____

_____

Nothing Can Separate Us

If God is for us, who can be against us? . . . Who shall
separate us from the love of Christ? . . . Neither death nor
life, neither angels nor demons, neither the present nor
the future, nor any powers, neither height nor depth, nor
anything else in all creation, will be able to separate us from
the love of God that is in Christ Jesus our Lord.

—ROMANS 8:31, 35, 38–39

Think about it: nothing in all creation can separate us from the love of God. No pain, heartache, disappointment, financial difficulty, or any other outward circumstance can ever change the degree or intensity of his care for us.

The apostle Paul was no stranger to suffering or trouble. When he lists things like hardship, persecution, famine, danger, or sword, he isn't speaking theoretically. He's talking about the kinds of trials he himself experienced. Just read his catalogue of suffering in 2 Corinthians 11:24–28. This could be called his interim report, the disasters that had already happened to him long before his execution at the hands of the Romans.

So we aren't getting cheap advice from some armchair theologian, but from an on-site missionary who had been through it all many times before. It's hard to meet someone confronted with such an unbelievable variety of calamities. Yet it's hard to find anyone who remained so positive throughout life, not merely in spite of them but because of them.

What kept the great apostle going? It was simply the

overwhelming conviction that, whatever came his way, he was eternally safe and secure in the love of God. Nothing could really touch him. Nothing could dislodge his position with God the Father and Jesus his Son. He was able to laugh in the face of trial and tribulation only because it couldn't really get to the center of his being. Every time he lost something valuable in this life, he knew that day by day he was getting closer to his homeland, the kingdom that couldn't be shaken.

So how do we come to that same confidence? By going through life's troubles and coming out of them in one piece. When we pass through the storms and live to tell others about it, we grow another inch in spiritual stature. If it doesn't happen, if all we ever experience is smooth seas and mild weather, then we will be of no use to others who are struggling to get through. So it's not just about us. God wants us to become positive, strong people for the sake of others.

TODAY'S PRAYER

Pray that God will show you all the various ways your present struggle will lead the way to your personal faith growth. Pray also that God will make you a great encouragement to those around you who are struggling to hang on and desperately need a visible witness to God's faithfulness.

TODAY'S PROGRESS

_____

_____

_____

_____

Searched and Known

O Lord, you have searched me and you know me. You know
when I sit and when I rise; you perceive my thoughts from
afar. You discern my going out and my lying down; you are
familiar with all my ways. Before a word is on my tongue
you know it completely, O Lord. You hem me in—behind
and before; you have laid your hand upon me.

–PSALM 139:1–5

Once again, we are facing what is, for some people, the most terrifying of all aspects of the Maker of heaven and earth. He knows every microscopic fact of our lives. He sees everything we're doing, saying, and thinking, and he knows it all even before we do. Of course, if we're doing, saying, and thinking things we shouldn't be, we cringe at the thought of God's depth of knowledge.

But if we're intending and making every effort to live according to his will, even if we blow it on a daily basis, then we can take great pleasure in the image of the watchful parent over the child. What normal, healthy parent scowls at the child and gets angry when she stumbles and falls when trying to walk? What parent doesn't take pleasure in observing each movement of the infant? If we fallen creatures know how to enjoy taking care of our children, how much more does our Maker enjoy taking care of us!

"But I don't like the way God is taking care of me right now!" Neither does the little child who wants his will more than the bear wants honey or the dog wants the meat you're eating at the table. We don't have to like every minute of it. We need only know that at every moment God has our best interests in mind and won't give in no matter how hard we beg, groan, or complain about him.

We can rejoice that God has total power and always gets his way in the end. The good news is that in God, and only in God, does absolute power combine with absolute goodness.

Truly, as the psalmist says, we are hemmed in. When God decides to lay his hand upon us, he does so with unqualified, unflinching commitment and with a purpose that is unwavering. That's a fact we can relax in.

TODAY'S PRAYER

Is God not letting you get your way? Express to him your gratitude for his unflagging commitment to your good. Then pray for a new freedom and strength to let go of the personal disappointment at your current struggle.

TODAY'S PROGRESS

_____

_____

_____

_____

_____

_____

Real Security

He who dwells in the shelter of the Most High will rest in
the shadow of the Almighty. I will say of the Lord, "He
is my refuge and my fortress, my God, in whom I trust."
Surely he will save you from the fowler's snare and from
the deadly pestilence. He will cover you with his feathers,
and under his wings you will find refuge; his faithfulness
will be your shield and rampart.

–PSALM 91:1–4

Psalm 91 gives us a number of very comforting images, each one chosen to maximize our sense of security in God. Just think carefully about each one:

- You can dwell in the shelter of the Most High.
- You can rest in the shadow of the Almighty.
- He is your refuge and your fortress.
- He will save you from the fowler's snare and from the deadly pestilence.
- He will cover you with his feathers, and under his wings you will find refuge.
- His faithfulness will be your shield and rampart.

It's as though if we don't get the point of one, the psalmist presents another—if the imagery of one doesn't grab us, maybe the next one will.

If we were to translate this passage into something more contemporary, we could list things such as: underground bomb shelter, impenetrable bunker, fail-safe security system, faithful-to-death bodyguard . . . and the list goes on. Many of the greatest images of safety and security were gathered here to communicate to us the wonderful oversight of our Creator.

The psalmist shows us how we really get away from fear and find the peace of mind we seek. We get all this by doing what the Bible tells us repeatedly to do—to dwell in God, trusting in him. "To dwell" means to abide or to remain or to continue. It is found all throughout the Bible and is a favorite way in the New Testament of expressing the life of faith (see John 15:1–17). It means that if we want to live in a place of safety and security, then we need to unpack our bags, throw our lot in with Jesus, and plan to live out our lives unreservedly under the umbrella of God's will and purpose. It's in this that we will find our joy, purpose, and confidence. Those who have done this for the long haul have found it to be true. You can be one of them.

TODAY'S PRAYER

Think about your greatest fear today. Now ask God to overwhelm you with a sense of absolute security in his protective care and let him dwarf your fear in light of his powerful presence.

TODAY'S PROGRESS

_____

_____

_____

_____

Set Free

In my anguish I cried to the Lord, and he answered by
setting me free. The Lord is with me; I will not be afraid.
What can man do to me?

−PSALM 118:5−6

It would be difficult to calculate the number of times in the
Bible we find the theme that someone cried out to God and
was delivered and set free. That's really the central message of
both Testaments—freedom! Freedom from all that oppresses,
all that harms, all that sends us into despair and disillusionment and final destruction.

The quintessential deliverance event of the Old Testament
is that of Moses and the exodus from Egypt. The central feature
of the New Testament message is Jesus' sacrificial death and
resurrection. Everything else in between is just commentary.
How to get freedom from slavery and death is the big picture
and the main story of the Bible.

When we pray desperately for release from some form of
earthly bondage, we're actually in a long line of those who have
gone before us and done the same thing. God wants us to reach
the same unshakable conviction as they and the psalmist who
said, "The Lord is with me; I will not be afraid. What can man
do to me?" This is the nature of fearlessness offered to those
who trust God. It was taught by Jesus and is reaffirmed by the
apostles in their letters and journals, by all the early believers,
the Reformers, missionaries, and anyone of faith we choose to
interview today in any part of the world.

So cry out to the Lord about your pain, your frustration, your anguish, your sorrow, and trust in him to deliver and comfort you in his way and time. It may be true that you're slogging through at the moment with troubles and enemies of all kinds surrounding you, but know that you are actually moving forward toward a brighter day, simply because it's God who is your Guide on the journey and the Lord of tomorrow.

TODAY'S PRAYER

Express to God your grateful confidence that whatever bondage or captivity you face today, freedom is on the way. Take heart in the fact that nothing can stop it.

TODAY'S PROGRESS

_____

_____

_____

_____

_____

_____

_____

_____

_____

Light and Momentary Troubles

Therefore we do not lose heart. Though outwardly we are wasting away, yet inwardly we are being renewed day by day. For our light and momentary troubles are achieving for us an eternal glory that far outweighs them all. So we fix our eyes not on what is seen, but on what is unseen. For what is seen is temporary, but what is unseen is eternal.

–2 CORINTHIANS 4:16–18

If we really want to know what Paul means here, all we have to do is look in the mirror. Day by day, the process of disintegration goes on. Nothing can stop it. Nothing can slow it down for long. As hard as we try to beat it back—all the creams, surgeries, and exercises will help for a short time—in the end, nature will have its way with us.

I decided that by my fiftieth birthday I would, by sheer self-discipline and rigorous dedication and training, be transformed into a finely tuned, lean and mean martial arts machine. To make a long story short, things didn't work out quite the way I'd hoped. I didn't become, as planned, a lean, mean martial arts machine. Instead I ended up a graying, middle-aged Presbyterian minister with broken ribs! Very unwillingly, I came nose to nose with reality.

So what can we say when we see our outward forms decaying and wasting away? What should our response be? Cry and moan and make other people around us miserable in the process? No, the only right response to aging and death is to look in the mirror and laugh at it. We need to learn to mock it and say, "You can't do anything to me because every day you take me down a notch further, I'm being renewed on the inside. And when the time comes that this body doesn't last through the night, I'll be clothed in a body that can't be touched by pain, aging, or weakness any longer."

In comparison to what is coming, our "light and momentary troubles" are really nothing. Our destiny far outweighs our present. So we can live through each day just as Paul did and just as our ancestors did, keeping our eyes on the unseen, the coming kingdom of God that has already broken powerfully into our darkness and proved itself real and lasting. God gives us just enough tokens of the glory to come to enable us to get through anything this world can throw at us.

TODAY'S PRAYER

With God's help, imagine yourself laughing in the face of every form of decay, disintegration, and loss. Now ask God to supply you with the ability to see beyond the temporary and hold fast to the solid hope of resurrection life.

TODAY'S PROGRESS

_____

_____

_____

_____

_____

Lenses

The LORD foils the plans of the nations; he thwarts the purposes of the peoples. But the plans of the LORD stand firm forever, the purposes of his heart through all generations.

—PSALM 33:10–11

What better news can there be than this? Few of us remember the terrors of years past—the Great Depression, world wars, concentration camps, the threat of global tyranny, ruthless armies marching across entire continents. So to most of us who have grown up in post World War II America or Europe, the seeming chaos of today sends waves of fear through us.

Instead of being afraid, let's turn to God and learn to look through the lenses he gives us when we come to trust in him. When we do, we immediately notice that things aren't always what they seem. If it appears that we are all at the mercy of others and their agendas—the pawns of political and military leaders, parliaments, congresses, banks, human institutions and plans, even family members or those we thought friends—this is all just show. We aren't in their hands, but God's.

Whatever plans and purposes may be hatched in the backrooms, boardrooms, war rooms, or government chambers of the world, they will be allowed only if they fit into the overarching purposes and plans of our Creator. He grants approval (or not) to each one.

God is not a God of caprice or chance. He moves by purpose and design every step of the way, and nothing ultimately stops or frustrates his plans. It may appear for a while that the schemes of evil people or nations are being fulfilled without any resistance, but at the end of the day God will use their evil for his good purposes. They may enjoy success for a while, but it's not for long.

The Bible teaches us that there's a special power acting in the world that keeps evil on a leash. Remember in the first pages of this book, the Holy Spirit was described as hovering over the unruly and chaotic mass during creation. The Spirit "brooded over" the chaos and extracted order from it. He's done so throughout every generation and continues to do so this very day. This is our security in the midst of all evil, social or political unrest, and our personal hard times.

TODAY'S PRAYER

If you find that your days are becoming darker and more fear filled, ask God to clear away the fog of doubt and anxiety and to grant you the ability to see that, even in the greatest storm, it is he who is behind the gale driving you to his perfectly planned destination.

TODAY'S PROGRESS

_____

_____

_____

_____

_____

_____

Overflow with Hope

*May the God of hope fill you with all joy and peace as you
trust in him, so that you may overflow with hope by the
power of the Holy Spirit.*

—ROMANS 15:13

Do you know what it's like to overflow with hope? Have you ever experienced it? There's one thing for sure—if you ever have experienced it, it's the work of God's Holy Spirit. Just take a look at most of the faces around you and see what you find. Hope? Joy? Love? Excitement about the days ahead? Probably not.

No, overflowing hope and joy are the products of God's presence. We can find a unique happiness and unmatched hope for the future only among those who have a solid reason to believe that the future is good—the Christians, not just the routine churchgoers or the religious-speak ones but the real ones, those who have the Spirit of Jesus living inside them.

There's a very close connection in the New Testament between God's Spirit and the presence of peace and joy. Where his Spirit invades, the gifts of his kingdom become evident to everyone, even unbelievers. And where real peace and joy reign, they bring the fruit of hope.

This hope grows steadily as we grow to trust in a loving God. There's a teeter-totter relationship between trust and hope that's easy to observe. When our trust in God is high, our despair and distress are low, and when our trust is low, our despair rises. So as we go through life and its turmoil learning to trust God more, we gain a deep sense of hope for the future.

Let's learn to ride the waves of adversity hand-in-hand with God and to let him lead us each time to safe harbor. Every time we come through another storm, we're actually increasing our hope quotient and so adding another solid reason to lead a genuinely joyful life.

And, by the way, every time we come through another storm successfully, we gain even more attention from our unbelieving or skeptical neighbors and give them even more reasons to think that our faith is something worth having.

TODAY'S PRAYER

Never forget there is no greater word of hope anywhere on earth than the gospel of Jesus. Pray that the Holy Spirit will bring you the gift of joyful hope even before the day God answers your prayers.

TODAY'S PROGRESS

Plans That Never Fall Through

"I know that you can do all things; no plan of
yours can be thwarted."

–JOB 42:2

This short passage has two very important things packed into it. First, it means what the rest of the Bible means when it says that God can do anything he wants without exception; and second, it means that what he does is directly connected to his design. In other words, he has plans, and nothing on this earth can stop, derail, delay, or preempt them. Nothing.

This is a foundational idea in the Bible and is exactly what it sounds like—with God nothing is impossible or out of his reach, and when he has decreed or planned something, there is no power that can frustrate him in carrying it out. If he chooses to change course, that's one thing, but if he does, it's not because he can't accomplish what he planned and is looking for some other way. He isn't like us. His ways are deeper, wider, and higher than ours, and he can't be measured by our standards or limitations.

We are so conditioned by our own experience of life that it's hard to imagine anything else. We plan, strategize, and strive to reach our goals, yet we're frustrated in the attempt by a hundred different things. So we go back to the drawing board and come up with another plan or way of getting it done.

Not so with God. What he plans, then announces, then

goes to work in bringing to fruition will occur just as he determined. What he promises will happen. What he says is as pure as highly refined silver. There's no equivocation, no backpedaling, no deceit. If God says that he rescues us by his own planning and decree, that nothing can snatch us from his hands, or that he'll be totally faithful to us in all circumstances, then it's one hundred percent true. What he promises will come true even if it means a lifetime of waiting.

Most of our prayers are consciously or unconsciously based on some clear promise made by God in Scripture. We ask for things because we have solid reasons for thinking that he'll grant them. So don't let anything take away your motivation to keep praying, asking, and waiting, because your ground for staying the course is stronger and more solid than anything else you can find in this life. Don't worry—if it's good for us and fits his plan for us, it's a done deal. If not, he'll protect us even from our greatest desires.

TODAY'S PRAYER

Do you keep laying your plans at Jesus' feet then picking them up again and trying to do things your way? Ask him to give you the patience to wait for his best plans and the ability to trust him to bring them about no matter how long it takes.

TODAY'S PROGRESS

Don't Stop

Be joyful always; pray continually; give thanks in all
circumstances, for this is God's will for you in Christ Jesus.

-1 THESSALONIANS 5:16-18

If you've been praying a long time about something or someone, then there's probably a very good reason for it. Something's not right or not the way you think it should be. If so, Paul is telling you something you need to know. Pray continually, and be always joyful. Give thanks in all circumstances.

Notice he didn't say give thanks *for* all circumstances, as if we're supposed to enjoy or want trouble or distress. But giving thanks in all situations means to offer our appreciation to God regardless of what's happening to us at the moment, even if we don't like it, even if it's the exact opposite of what we prayed for. Such exercises of discipline show that we're acknowledging that God's will and ideas for us are better than ours. We don't have to like our circumstances, but we can thank God for whatever he is accomplishing in us through them. This is, he says, God's will for us in Christ Jesus.

It's the goal of a lifetime to learn this one great lesson: God's will is always better than ours. His ways are always and in every case higher than ours, and he wants us to get the point that the best and highest prayer we can ever pray is, "Let your will be done."

We aren't Buddhists who are taught to desire less. Rather we are Christians who are taught to desire more. For in desiring more, we realize that God's will really is better than ours and that it's only in the desiring more that we ever find it.

When the time is right and if it's for our good and in his will, then he will bring about our desires, often even above and beyond what we're praying for.

TODAY'S PRAYER

List all the trials that God has sent your way or that you are going through today and praise him for every one of them. Thank him again that he cares enough to tailor-make daily experiences for your growth and to draw you into his eternal good purposes.

TODAY'S PROGRESS

_____

_____

_____

_____

_____

_____

_____

_____

_____

_____

Behind the Scenes

For our struggle is not against flesh and blood, but against
the rulers, against the authorities, against the powers of
this dark world and against the spiritual forces of evil in the
heavenly realms. Therefore put on the full armor of God, so
that when the day of evil comes, you may be able to stand
your ground, and after you have done everything, to stand.

−EPHESIANS 6:12–13

This passage flies directly in the face of what most modern, "enlightened" people who don't believe in evil think about the world and its problems. It also sheds light on why we pray. If all our struggles were simply against humans and all their plots and schemes, then we could oppose them with plots and schemes even more clever than theirs. It would be just a matter of who had the best strategy.

But Paul wants us to understand that this simple, two-dimensional view of things is not only wrong, it's actually dangerously wrong. If we launch out in life with our home-made, incomplete ideas on what makes people tick, in total ignorance of the unseen spiritual powers behind the scenes, we'll end up falling flat on our faces. Guaranteed failure awaits the person who is blind to the spiritual dimension yet tries to solve the serious problems of life.

Fortunately, we have a vital defense against these powers: prayer. We pray because we recognize that we can't do things on our own steam, with our own intelligence and expertise. It usually takes years to learn this lesson, but the sooner the better.

When we're praying, we can't afford to forget that behind the physical world, behind the human and earthly, are the principalities and powers pulling the strings. These spiritual forces are too strong for any of us no matter how spiritual we think we are, but they're no match for the Holy Spirit, our advocate and defender.

So whatever it is we're bringing before God in petition or intercession, let's do so by putting on the whole armor of God so that, when the day of evil comes, we will be able to stand our ground.

TODAY'S PRAYER

Are you confused about what is happening to you? Do you feel like you're walking around in a fog? Then pray, pray, pray. And pray some more. Ask God to give you the wisdom to discern the spirits that are creating this confusion and to burn away the fog that is penetrating your mind. Pray for the Holy Spirit to protect and shield you and your loved ones.

TODAY'S PROGRESS

_____

_____

_____

_____

_____

_____

_____

Suffering and Comfort

Praise be to the God and Father of our Lord Jesus Christ,
the Father of compassion and the God of all comfort, who
comforts us in all our troubles, so that we can comfort those
in any trouble with the comfort we ourselves have received
from God. For just as the sufferings of Christ flow over into
our lives, so also through Christ our comfort overflows.

–2 CORINTHIANS 1:3–5

Statements like these confront life head-on. Paul is very aware that just as Jesus Christ suffered in this world, so will we suffer, often simply because we're his followers. But just as we suffer with him, so will God comfort us by him. As the Father loved the Son and comforted him in his sorrows, so he stands by to encourage and sustain us. This is the consistent testimony of believers for the last two thousand years.

But the circle doesn't end there. Just as God lifted up his Son and lifts us up in our troubles, so we are equipped to lift up other people around us who suffer. Where does the power come from to care deeply about others when we're so inclined to think only of ourselves and our own troubles? It comes once again by the Holy Spirit who dwells with and in us.

This is pretty easy to prove in real life. As we look around the world, whom do we find lending a helping hand to the downtrodden and needy? Who are the people right there on the scene when disaster strikes, or who rush to the refugees and the wounded? By and large, they are those who have been comforted themselves by God the Father through Jesus the Son. It's most often the followers of Jesus who sacrifice their own lives and careers to help the broken and dispossessed. It's most often the heavenly minded who do the most earthly good.

All this work in the world is the product of God's serving us first. We serve because we've been served. We give because we've been given. And we have every reason to move forward in this world with the confidence that, when trouble comes our way again, the unending mercy of God will be there every time.

TODAY'S PRAYER

Are you overwhelmed by your pain and suffering? First, confess to God your anguish and ask him to grant you the same peace and comfort that he gave to his Son, our Savior. Know that no matter what you are going through, Jesus has already been there before you and is with you now to help you through your pain. Then ask God to help you be a source of comfort to those around you.

TODAY'S PROGRESS

_____

_____

_____

_____

_____

_____

Are You Listening?

I call on you, O God, for you will answer me; give
ear to me and hear my prayer.

–PSALM 17:6

Have you ever wondered whether God was actually listening to you when you prayed? And did you ever voice your concern? If so, you're in good company—the company of complainers! There were a number of psalmists apart from King David who recorded their complaints. And many of them were quite open about their frustration over the seeming silence of heaven and the apparent "earlessness" of God. The people of God in general often wondered if God was listening to them or was even aware of their plight. But on one occasion God responded through the psalmist by asking the question: "Does he who implanted the ear not hear?" (Ps. 94:9).

Great counterquestion! Since it was God who designed and created the ear in the first place, how is it that we think he does not or cannot hear? Seems kind of silly, doesn't it? Not only does God hear every word spoken every moment by every human being on earth, he also knows every thought and every motivation behind every thought (1 Chron. 28:9). That's not good news to those who don't want there to be a God, but very good news to those who do.

So it's absolutely certain that God is "lending an ear" when we pray. The writer of this particular psalm is convinced (most likely on the basis of long experience) that God will hear him when he calls and that God will answer him.

Let's join him in that conviction by shaking off the recurring fear that the heavens are silent and by expecting that the God who knows all there is to know is well aware of our need, hears our voice, and will fulfill his good plan and purpose for us. He may take his time in answering, but he will arrive on schedule.

TODAY'S PRAYER

Are you wondering if God gave you the gift of complaint? If yes, be assured that you aren't the first person to think so. Acknowledge your weakness, then ask God to remove your fear and replace it with the knowledge of his ever-abiding presence in your life.

TODAY'S PROGRESS

_____

_____

_____

_____

_____

_____

_____

_____

_____

Reality Therapy

*Brothers, we do not want you to be ignorant about those who
fall asleep, or to grieve like the rest of men, who have no hope.*

–1 THESSALONIANS 4:13

Even though Paul is talking about those who were grieving
over their loved ones who had died, the point remains the
same about grief over anything lost: dreams, hopes, friends,
jobs, finances, relationships.

But why shouldn't we grieve over anything the way the rest
of the world grieves? Because of the hope we have in Jesus. For
the follower of Jesus, grief is based only on a temporary loss.
The sense of ultimate tragedy shouldn't be present among our
family and loved ones.

There was a story on the news of a soldier reported killed in
action. The family was officially informed of his death and was
immediately plunged into great sorrow. But just a few days later,
the military reported that a mistake had been made and it was
not their son, but someone else, who had been killed.

The family's grief at the time was real, but it was based on a
false understanding of the true situation. It's the same way when
we experience the death of a departed loved one in the faith. For
sure we experience sorrow over the loss, but it is not the sorrow
of ultimate loss or the sorrow based on a false view of life. We
hold firmly to the hope (meaning confident assurance) of being
with that loved one again, this time forever.

But how is hope for this distant life beyond the grave related
to your 100-day prayer? Here's the point: the same hope applies

to the loss of anything, maybe the very thing you're praying about right now. There's nothing we can lose in this world that cannot be restored—absolutely nothing. If it's capable of being lost, it's capable of being recovered, either in this life or the next.

Let that stay in the forefront of your mind when you're praying about anything you think has been snatched unjustly or abruptly from you. Practice some "reality therapy" in the situation you're facing. The reality of the resurrection isn't only an encouragement just for the end of the world. It's supposed to affect everything we think about and do today. The same power that operated to raise Jesus' physical body from the tomb on Easter morning is operating this very day to bring dead things back to life: dead dreams, dead careers, dead marriages, and all the rest. This good news is the very heart of the faith—don't forget it!

TODAY'S PRAYER

Are you afraid that you are never going to get over your loss? Then open up your Bible and read again about Jesus' resurrection from the dead, and remember that God can and does use that same power in your life today as he did in the past.

TODAY'S PROGRESS

_____

_____

_____

_____

_____

The Story's Not Over

*I have learned to be content whatever the circumstances. I know
what it is to be in need, and I know what it is to have plenty. I have
learned the secret of being content in any and every situation,
whether well fed or hungry, whether living in plenty or in want. I
can do everything through him who gives me strength.*

–PHILIPPIANS 4:11–13

During these one hundred days of prayer, it's very likely that
what we're facing is a situation of want—job security, financial difficulties, relationships, family—and it's easy to succumb
to despair. If so, keep this in mind: Jesus is sufficient for whatever
is happening. He may not choose to release us from our problem
at this particular time. Deliverance may lie in the future. But
whether what we want comes to us today or tomorrow, or many
tomorrows from now, we can reach a balance and rest from the
stress of it when we learn to find our place of security in him. In
fact, this may be the purpose of the training period we're going
through right now.

We reach this place of security with God's help. Life lived
in Jesus Christ works a different way. If we live, we live in and
for Jesus. If we die, we die in Jesus. If we are prosperous or in
need, we live for Jesus in whatever circumstances are decreed
for us. These fluctuations of life merely teach us in the most
graphic way that this world isn't our home. We don't have to
like it!

Soldiers in boot camp aren't fully aware of what the rigors
of training are preparing them for, but they find out later when

they face the fierce heat of battle. Without that training, they would certainly perish.

So hang in there. The story isn't over. We are being trained to live a life that brings glory to God and great blessing to us, and we can do anything or go through anything if we know there's a purpose to it. Does this mean that we stop praying or hoping for deliverance and rescue, for joy, peace, and abundance? No, we just realize that, at the proper time (hopefully soon!), God will bring to pass what we need and what he wants. Between now and then, we learn to be content in our discontentment.

Don't forget what Paul says just a few verses later in Philippians: "And my God will meet all your needs according to his glorious riches in Christ Jesus" (4:19).

TODAY'S PRAYER

Alongside your prayer for the particular request that occupies this 100-day period, pray for the "interim gift," the supernatural gift of contentment in the midst of want. God loves to grant it.

TODAY'S PROGRESS

_____

_____

_____

_____

_____

_____

Valley of the Shadow

Even though I walk through the valley of the shadow of death, I will fear no evil, for you are with me; your rod and your staff, they comfort me.

−PSALM 23:4

If the promises of God aren't related to the reality of death, then they aren't of much use to us. Death should hold no ultimate terror to the child of God simply because God is Lord of all life, from beginning to end, and beyond.

But the psalmist is not talking here about the one who dies, but the one who doesn't! He's referring to the threat of death, the nearness of it, the valley of death. To the one who's been there or is there now, it needs no further definition or explanation. King David had plenty of occasions to write this psalm because he had more than his share of near-death experiences. People who were only too willing to help him into the grave before his appointed day (and would have had a very enjoyable time doing so) often surrounded him. He was no stranger to evil in all its forms, particularly in its human form—spitefulness, betrayal, violence, duplicity, slander, and all the rest.

So this psalm celebrates that aspect of God's character that permits us to walk through the valley of the shadow of death but makes sure that death doesn't strike us. He uses the imagery of the shepherd's life since it was in his own experience of shepherding real sheep that he grew in his understanding of his powerful Creator. There were dangers around every corner for the shepherd, and more than once David faced certain death

(1 Sam. 17:34–37). Yet as he passed through the many valleys under death's shadow, he was learning the ways of God and was comforted by God's abiding presence. Through this daily walk, he grew to fear no evil simply because he faced it so many times and lived to tell of his Creator's rescuing power.

So where's the good news for us? It's this: God is the God of all life and of all our lives. He allows us to walk into and through the valley to train us in the same way he trained David. He's showing us his mercy and saving power so that we'll trust him more on the next trip. There is no evil to fear on this earth because he permits no more of it than we can face at any given time, and he brings us victoriously through it all.

When in his wisdom and providence he decrees that real death will meet us in the valley, it still holds no terror for us believers because in Jesus Christ the sting of death has been removed (1 Cor. 15:55).

TODAY'S PRAYER

Usually we have more than one thing to pray for. It's okay to ask God for daily protection from all forms of peril under death's shadow along with our main need or desire.

TODAY'S PROGRESS

_____

_____

_____

_____

_____

The Perfect Plan

If we ask anything according to his will, he hears us. And if we know that he hears us—whatever we ask—we know that we have what we asked of him.

−1 JOHN 5:14−15

Here in this passage is the answer to the perennial question: What did Jesus mean when he said that we'll have whatever we ask in his name? Obviously he didn't mean what it sounds like on the surface of things. If that were true, we would have that new car, vacation home, or big end-of-the-year bonus every time we asked. So much strange Bible teaching has come from the idea that if we pray in just the right way or use just the right words then God will open the floodgates of heaven.

But remember, what it really means to ask for things "in the name of Jesus" is not merely to tack on that phrase at the end of our prayer, as if it's some magic incantation. Rather it's to ask according to God's perfect will. We need to put our theologies together by looking at the entire body of Scripture, not just quoting one single passage as if it explained everything. The statement in John 15 is clarified by the same writer in 1 John 5:14−15, and the two should be read together.

When we become the kind of people who prefer God's will over ours, even though we may want what we want very intensely (which isn't wrong), God will say yes more often than he says no. He wants what he wants even more than we want what we want, because he knows that what he intends for us is better in the long run than what we dream about for ourselves.

So let this be your North Star as you're praying. Tell God your deepest longings, knowing that they may really be in line with his will (sometimes our dreams are put there by God in the first place), but leave open the possibility that his plan is still greater and may lead more directly to your desired destination.

TODAY'S PRAYER

Think about the real "Lord's Prayer," the prayer he prayed in the Garden of Gethsemane before his crucifixion. Its essence was this: "Your will be done." He repeated it three times. It's the best way to pray for something, anything. Say it often and with real conviction.

TODAY'S PROGRESS

_____

_____

_____

_____

_____

_____

_____

_____

_____

He Stills the Storm

He stilled the storm to a whisper; the waves of the sea were
hushed. They were glad when it grew calm, and he guided
them to their desired haven.

–PSALM 107:29–30

This verse occurs in a long discourse recalling all the good things God had done for those who trusted him. It was typical of the Hebrews, who constantly remembered their history, to be forever reminding their children of it. And this catalogue of shared stories was the glue that kept people together from generation to generation. It works the same way today; that's why it's important for families and congregations to remember and pass on the details of things they've gone through together.

In the Bible, the storm was a common example and symbol of chaos and distress. The image of the tiny vessel being tossed to and fro on the churning sea was a very useful picture of human life at the mercy of forces beyond our control. The intent here is not just the fact that God has control of nature and the elements (see the parallel account of Jesus quelling the storm in Mark 4:35–41) but that God has everything in his hands and brings us to our desired haven even by means of the storm. Every storm is God's storm. The apostle Paul affirms the same truth when he says that "in all things God works for the good of those who love him, who have been called according to his purpose" (Rom. 8:28).

So once again we have the promise of God's superintending care over all of life. The Bible says the same thing over and over again just because we forget it over and over again! It reminds us that whatever happens to us is no surprise to God and he is never in a quandary over what to do about it. He has written our life's script and pronounced it very good. No matter what it looks like at the moment, as we keep our eyes fixed on Jesus, he will either calm the storm or lead us through it to safety.

TODAY'S PRAYER

Whatever it is you're asking from God, again keep in mind that he uses needs to drive us to places we wouldn't otherwise go. Thank him once again for whatever he is doing that you can't see at the moment.

TODAY'S PROGRESS

_____

_____

_____

_____

_____

_____

_____

_____

All Kinds of Problems

In this you greatly rejoice, though now for a little while
you may have had to suffer grief in all kinds of trials.
These have come so that your faith—of greater worth than
gold, which perishes even though refined by fire—may be
proved genuine and may result in praise, glory and honor
when Jesus Christ is revealed.

–1 PETER 1:6–7

Do we like to suffer grief in all kinds of trials? Absolutely not! Do we rejoice greatly when they come? Who would?! But rejoicing seems to be what Peter is telling us to do—and not only to rejoice but to rejoice greatly! In this I'm sure he doesn't expect us to be thrilled by the suffering but thrilled that God is doing something in us by it.

Actually, there's nothing quite like trouble to get us on our knees. What we need to know about our struggles is that they come to us for a purpose. They're not just accidents that fall upon us without God's knowledge or permission. They come by decree, by divine appointment, and with high purpose. Peter tells us that just as gold is refined by an exceedingly hot purifying process, so we are refined and outfitted for eternity by the things that happen to us here on earth.

We don't have to like the process by which we get there, but we will love the result of it when it's done. And by the way, the apostle Paul tells us that whatever suffering we may experience in this life is too minuscule to measure when compared to the future glory that awaits us (Rom. 8:18).

Also, both Paul and Peter remind us that what we do suffer on this earth is just for a little while. While our trials are temporary and comparatively brief, our joy and happiness are eternal.

Peter tells us later in his letter (5:7) that because God cares for us, we have the privilege of casting upon God all the anxiety caused by our troubles. He is more than able to carry the things we can't and aren't really designed to carry. So however hot the fire, we can rejoice that God is with us in the furnace and through it is accomplishing something real and lasting.

TODAY'S PRAYER

If you're finding that the weight of carrying the burden of your need is too great, then be happy that you've gotten the point. Now ask God to teach you what it means for him to carry what you can't.

TODAY'S PROGRESS

_____

_____

_____

_____

_____

_____

_____

History Therapy

Many, O Lᴏʀᴅ my God, are the wonders you have done. The
things you planned for us no one can recount to you; were I to
speak and tell of them, they would be too many to declare.

–PSALM 40:5

Today let's begin a new spiritual discipline we can call "history therapy." It works like this. Take a note pad and pen and sit down alone at some quiet place. Think back as far as you can and try to remember the very first thing you'd regard as a sign of God intervening in your life. Write down anything that might even border on what you'd classify as a "God-event." Maybe it's a last-minute rescue, being snatched from a fire or grabbed before you sank in a pool or lake. Maybe you were healed from some fatal illness or an amazing coincidence changed the course of your life.

As the days pass and you recall different events, keep adding them to your growing "God-event" list. Now include those rescues of your friends, relatives, church relationships, and neighbors as you remember them.

Okay, now let's turn to the Bible. People in the Bible aren't merely interesting historical personalities—they're members of our family, and the Bible is our family album. In it we see that the things we go through are very much like what they endured. We are part of their story, and they are part of ours. This is the bond that ties us all together, for God tends to work, rescue, and help in the same way today as he has so many times before.

So what is written in the Bible is written not just for "way back then" but also for and to us (Rom. 15:4). When we put together the list we have created for our own lives and add to that the long list of rescues and deliverances of many others, we have an enormous weight of evidence testifying to God's involvement with people in every generation.

As we mature in our faith and our spiritual eyesight improves, we'll be able to look back and see God's hand in all of our life. With "history therapy," we'll learn to relax and know for sure that God is in charge. It will finally sink into our minds and hearts that he is involved (and always has been) in our struggles, and we can know that it's really irrational and unreasonable to think that God has abandoned us, because we would have to deny all our personal history as well as years of world history to believe he doesn't act for us. And if he was with us then, he'll be with us now and every day forever after.

TODAY'S PRAYER

Ask God for enlightenment. Pray for him to open your mind and quicken your memory in order to see all the various ways and means he has used (even the more hidden ones) to bless you and keep you through the years of your life.

TODAY'S PROGRESS

_____

_____

_____

_____

_____

The Higher Order

"For my thoughts are not your thoughts, neither are your ways my ways," declares the LORD. "As the heavens are higher than the earth, so are my ways higher than your ways and my thoughts than your thoughts."

–ISAIAH 55:8–9

We should be happy that God doesn't think about things exactly the way we do. Can you imagine how scary that would be?

The prophet Isaiah talks about what may be called "the higher order." If our faith is real, then it will lead to the recognition of a higher, wider, and deeper purpose and measure of things. Every believer eventually comes to the place where he or she recognizes what Isaiah heard, understood, and recorded for us—words that have grounded and stabilized believers for centuries.

This conviction of a higher order grows with each new advance of faith. With the passing of years comes new levels of spiritual maturity, and eventually we realize that there really is a higher way in the universe than what we learn from ordinary life. The experiences we go through, things that happen to us, people we meet from day to day, lessons we learn through every new trial, odd coincidences we observe, losses we suffer, advantages and promotions we enjoy—all of this is part of a purpose that transcends our own and points toward a well-thought-out plan and a destiny beyond the present earthly order. We can be sure that the meaning of many experiences in life will remain almost a complete mystery to us until we come to a place where they are allowed to unfold and make sense within the higher purpose.

Thank God there really is a higher order! This truth keeps us on track as we pray. It eventually makes sense of all the confusions and mysteries of prayer: the time involved in framing the real request and waiting for the answer, God's deliberate "delays" in coming to help, the apparent nos (or not yets) he gives to our requests, and all the related details surrounding our problems and their solutions. Everything happens to us and for us under this protective umbrella.

TODAY'S PRAYER

If you haven't done it yet, ask the Holy Spirit to do his favorite work: to reveal to you the reality of the higher order, and then thank God for the fact that there really is one. It'll make your day.

TODAY'S PROGRESS

_____

_____

_____

_____

_____

_____

Real Love

The LORD appeared to us in the past, saying: "I have
loved you with an everlasting love; I have drawn you
with loving-kindness."

–JEREMIAH 31:3

The same theme of Jeremiah 29 appears again here. God calls his people in captivity to return to their homeland to what he had intended for them in the first place. The motive for that plan was that God loved them with an everlasting love. It was his loving-kindness, not their spectacular obedience or performance, that drew them to him and that continued to hover over them even in their rebellion against him.

It's hard for us to imagine this kind of love. Parents can gain a little glimpse of it when love for their children remains strong in spite of their children's rebellion. But God goes even beyond that. He sustains his loving-kindness long after the last parent has given up on the last wayward child. Our love can grow cold, but God's love cannot. Our love is often conditional, but God's is not. True, we can reject his love, but his love is not thereby lessened. He still holds out his hand in our direction, and his ongoing patience is intended to lead us to repentance (Rom. 2:4).

The ultimate expression of this love for us is in the sending of his Son Jesus to reconcile us to himself and to bring us home. "For God so loved the world that he gave his one and only Son, that whoever believes in him shall not perish but have eternal life" (John 3:16). What this means for us is that whatever troubles and grief come our way, whatever betrayals and losses we experience, Jesus hangs on to us even when we can't hang on to him and brings us safely home.

So why are we secure? Because God keeps and blesses those who keep the rules and do the right thing all the time? No. We're safe because of God's loving-kindness and steadfast faithfulness.

TODAY'S PRAYER

Pray for God to open your mind so completely to this truth that you'll never think the same way again. Allow him to show you the many-sided, unshakeable love he has for you, a love that breaks all the barriers of how you've always defined the word before.

TODAY'S PROGRESS

_____

_____

_____

_____

_____

_____

_____

_____

Ask with Confidence

*For we do not have a high priest who is unable to
sympathize with our weaknesses, but we have one who
has been tempted in every way, just as we are—yet was
without sin. Let us then approach the throne of grace with
confidence, so that we may receive mercy and find grace
to help us in our time of need.*

—HEBREWS 4:15–16

Whether we pray for one day, one hundred days, or one thousand days, let's do it the way God wants us to. We must be convinced that Jesus, who is the mediator between God and us, is not unmoved by our troubles or our many weaknesses. He was tempted in all the same general ways we are, yet he resisted to the very last and remained sinless. It's just not true that he doesn't know what we're going through. In fact, the blast of temptation was greater for him than for us because only the one who resists the temptation really knows how powerful it can be.

When we pray, we should come to God with great confidence that we will receive all the mercy and grace we could possibly want. It doesn't really matter how bad we've been or how thin our goodness has proved to be. God's program of salvation isn't based on how excellent our actions or faith has been; rather it comes directly out of the merciful character of our God.

God grants us grace and brings us our provisions simply because he likes to. We can ask him for anything, anything at all. He will answer and provide according to his plan for us, and he won't allow anything we ask for to get in the way of his best for us. If his answer is a no, then it's a no for our good, and if it's a yes, it's for our good too. We leave it up to our God to sort out the requests and do what is best. But God does expect us to ask and is pleased when we do. If we didn't ask for specific things, how would we ever know that he answers our prayers?

TODAY'S PRAYER

Banish from your mind the idea that God is so far away and so wrapped up in his celestial glory that he doesn't understand what it's like for you to live your life. Then thank him that you are permitted (commanded) to ask for what you want and need with boldness and reckless abandon.

TODAY'S PROGRESS

_____

_____

_____

_____

_____

_____

_____

_____

When God
Says No

Three times I pleaded with the Lord to take it away from
me. But he said to me, "My grace is sufficient for you, for my
power is made perfect in weakness." Therefore I will boast
all the more gladly about my weaknesses, so that Christ's
power may rest on me. That is why, for Christ's sake, I delight
in weaknesses, in insults, in hardships, in persecutions, in
difficulties. For when I am weak, then I am strong.

–2 CORINTHIANS 12:8–10

Anyone who's been praying for years knows that from time to time the heavens seem silent and we feel like no one is listening. But it's a feeling that comes and goes, and we shouldn't base our view of God on feelings. We'll always end up with a wrong understanding.

But there are occasions when God isn't silent and when the answer to our prayer seems to be a straightforward no. What then? How do we understand a direct no from God? Yes, it may be that a no is actually a not yet, but for all practical purposes, it's a no.

First let's look at it through the lens of Scripture. We know we're not in paradise yet, so we may assume that before we get there bad things can and will happen. It's like we're living behind enemy lines and life is the journey that brings us back home again.

We learn from Scripture that we live not for our own purposes and pleasures but for God's. Regardless of how often we hear the opposite message—that in this life we should be personally fulfilled at all costs—the truth is that we exist for God. We were created to bring honor and pleasure to him alone. If we exist for any other reason, we live in futility and ultimate disillusionment and despair.

Also we discover that often God gets more accomplished

with a no than a yes. If we had everything we asked for the minute we asked, then we probably wouldn't learn very much from the crisis of the moment. God teaches us to depend on him by means of trouble and difficulty. Otherwise, if things were always an easy skate across the ice, we would never grow spiritually. Let's face it, when things are going well, how easy is it to put God in the backseat and veer off on our own?

The apostle Paul learned only through his personal weaknesses how strong God was. God gave him a no to repeated prayers for deliverance just to keep him reliant on God's strength. It was one of the best answers to prayer Paul ever heard.

To some, this might seem like a mean and tyrannical God, someone who seems to delight in your pain and suffering. On the contrary, he's a gracious Father who wants only the very best for you. He knows what that is, and he's going to put you through whatever it takes to get you to that perfect place. So by saying no at this particular moment, he's actually saying yes to a lifetime of blessings and joy.

Nowhere Else to Go

*The LORD does whatever pleases him, in the heavens and on
the earth, in the seas and all their depths.*

–PSALM 135:6

This is another one of those places in the Bible that sort of
tosses ice water in our faces. Just when we begin to think
that we have all kinds of personal power and influence in the
world and over God, and all we have to do to make things
happen is to exercise our will as free beings, we hear the (unwel-
come) news that God is independent of all our choices and does
just exactly as he pleases. He doesn't have to do a single thing
we tell him to. (I know this goes against a great deal of Sunday
morning TV theology.)

This is the case wherever in the universe we go: in the heavens, on the earth, or in the depth of the seas. These are the
same places where David says that we can't flee to get out of
God's presence (Ps. 139:7–10). So he's not only there, he's there
in his total sovereignty. There's not a single place where God's
freedom is not operating.

So where's the rejoicing in all this? In the simple fact that
there could be no one more in our camp and ready to help, rescue, and bless than the One who does whatever he pleases. So
what pleases him? To give us everything he has. He is delighted
to hand over to us what he possesses—in this world and the next.

Does that mean we get whatever we want in life? No, he's
not so cruel. It means that we get whatever pleases him, namely,
whatever is good for us and is according to his good pleasure,

purpose, and plan. We can take comfort in the stubbornness of God, that part of his character that insists we arrive on the shores of his new heaven and new earth safe and sound, even if it means he has to say no to us ten thousand times in getting us there.

TODAY'S PRAYER

Have you ever thought of thanking and praising God for his sovereignty, the fact that he does whatever he wants? Since nothing could ever be better for us, get excited about it and ask God for a mature grasp of what it means. When you do get it, it'll change your life.

TODAY'S PROGRESS

_____

_____

_____

_____

_____

_____

_____

_____

Death Is Dead

I am the resurrection and the life. He who believes in
me will live, even though he dies; and whoever lives
and believes in me will never die.

—JOHN 11:25–26

What is evil's greatest weapon? What does every tyrant depend upon to secure power over others? Death. Death is the only final fact of this world, the irreversible event—the only one-way ticket. Death and the fear of it have reigned from the very beginning of human history to the present day. But should it for us?

The answer from the believer's point of view is no. Death no longer reigns over us, because Jesus came to defeat the final enemy. He did that on the cross, and in his resurrection, the tyrant's power is neutralized and fear is dispelled. On that Easter morning the new age dawned; his resurrection was the announcement that all creation would follow him. All that dies would live forever. What happened to his physical body would happen to the entire earth and to every person who wants to be part of the new heaven and the new earth predicted long before Jesus (Isa. 65 and 66) and reaffirmed in the New Testament (Matt. 19:28; Acts 3:21; Rom. 8:18–27; Rev. 21:1–4).

If the very worst thing that can happen to us has been defeated and overruled, then what about all the lesser things we worry about and dread? How many days or years do we spend in anxiety and fear of all the smaller things in life? If Jesus said

that all this is a total waste of time and produces nothing positive, let's get rid of it—today.

When we stop worrying about the smaller things, we come
to a strong confidence and trust in God for a final, wonderful
wrap-up specifically because he grants to us the many "little
resurrections" in this life. He demonstrates his resurrection
power through the numerous rescues, reversals, and deliverances we experience from now until the final rescue.

What he wants us to learn from these "pre-resurrections" is
that from the perspective of the resurrection, all fear, all anxiety, and all despair are absolutely unrealistic.

TODAY'S PRAYER

If you have cast aside your anxieties but are suddenly overwhelmed again by the desperateness of your situation, then toss
them aside once more. Ask God to rid your mind of every negative and hopeless thought and feeling, and trust him to bring
you to a joyful peace.

TODAY'S PROGRESS

_____

_____

_____

_____

_____

_____

_____

Foundation

*For no one can lay any foundation other than the one
already laid, which is Jesus Christ.*

–1 CORINTHIANS 3:11

After a tornado, there's not much left standing except for a few bricks, pipes, and pieces of concrete. The house is gone, with its windows, frame, roof, and all the rest. But if you take a closer look at the scene of devastation, what's the one thing left untouched? What is there that's still intact? The foundation. It's still there despite the enormous power of destruction that just passed through and annihilated everything in its path.

Foundations are there to stay when everything else goes. So it is with our faith walk—or faith building. Our foundation is not our faith; rather our faith is built upon the foundation of Jesus Christ. From a human point of view, our faith can ebb and flow like the tides—it may seem to us very high one day and very low or even non-existent the next, depending on circumstances, our health, or even body chemistry. Haven't you ever awakened one morning and felt that somehow all your faith had just drained out of you during the night?

So here's the good news: We don't have to create our own foundation. It's not up to us to support ourselves or sustain our own faith; it's not even totally up to us to remain faithful to God. It's God who lays the foundation, it's God who gives us the gift of faith, and it's God who hangs on to us and brings faith back when it fades, disappears, or is blown away in one of life's perfect storms.

Our faith is solid because our foundation is solid. It's based on the truth of Jesus' resurrection and backed by the gold of God's trustworthy character. We don't fear for the future because God will be the same reliable and faithful God tomorrow as he is today.

TODAY'S PRAYER

Do you feel that your faith flowed out with the last ebb tide? Then consider this truth that your faith is built on the foundation that is Jesus Christ. Thank God now that nothing can truly destroy your faith or separate you from him.

TODAY'S PROGRESS

_____

_____

_____

_____

_____

_____

_____

_____

_____

_____

Long and Winding Roads

Trust in the Lord with all your heart and lean not on your
own understanding; in all your ways acknowledge him,
and he will make your paths straight.

–PROVERBS 3:5–6

This is the kind of Scripture we like to quote regularly and then disregard immediately afterward. Every believer knows that we should trust in the Lord with all our heart and not lean on our own understanding, but when faced with something really extraordinary and inexplicable, something that goes way beyond our own ability to figure out, then the "trust in the Lord" part tends to get tossed out the window!

"What's all this about, Lord? This just doesn't make any sense at all. Where have you gone? Why have you forsaken me?" Sound familiar? Such questions reveal that we're still leaning on our own understanding. But the passage means exactly what it says: Don't lean on your understanding! Stop thinking that your view of things is all there is. If what you're going through right now doesn't make immediate sense, then assume without further fretfulness that this is the very situation referred to in the passage.

What's the solution? Acknowledge God in all your ways. Recognize and admit openly that he is in charge of everything and knows exactly what's at stake and what needs to be done. Confess his sovereignty over every detail of life and wait for him patiently to come and deliver you in his time and in his way. Remember your favorite hymns and songs of praise. Remind yourself of all that he has done for you in the past. Praise him and thank him that he is going to rescue and deliver you.

If we'll do that, the rest is up to him. It's his job, not ours, to make our paths straight. It's good to learn this lesson early. The sooner we can get this right, the sooner we can move forward and not have to keep repeating our course on Faith 101.

TODAY'S PRAYER

Are you feeling like you came to the crossroads and chose the wrong path? Ask God to help you get back on track and trust him to lead you back to the place of his promised blessing and deliverance.

TODAY'S PROGRESS

_____

_____

_____

_____

_____

_____

_____

_____

_____

_____

Dust in the Wind

*The world and its desires pass away, but the man who does
the will of God lives forever.*

–1 JOHN 2:17

Imagine—everything you see around you right now will eventually pass away. Everything. Every person, city, highway, automobile, scene, animal, home, and garden, plus every pain, sorrow, and evil. It's all going to vanish from the earth. We are in many ways just dust in the wind. That would be pretty depressing if it weren't for one vital piece of information: whoever does the will of God will live forever.

This is about as clear as it can possibly be. One of the main messages of the Bible is that there are only two ways: the way of life and the way of death. If we choose the way of life in Jesus Christ, we will live forever. But if we turn away and choose our own path, we'll fade away and disappear with everything else around us.

The knowledge that we'll die one day but not stay dead is fantastically important information. It means that life, not death, is God's last word to us. It means that whatever we're doing now and however it may turn out, it isn't the end of the matter. What we do in this life is important, but the greater is yet to come. Whatever we miss out on now is moderately (and temporarily) disappointing, but it's laughably inconsequential compared to the fact that nothing lost in this life is unrecoverable and nothing truly good that disappears will stay gone.

So when you're praying about that critical issue before you, just keep in mind that whatever the outcome, the last chapter of the book and the last act of the play are the only ones that really count. And the last act is the great wrap-up of the long story of how God intended from the first page to bring his people to incomparable glory, unimaginable joy, and indescribable fulfillment. This truth, discovered by millions before you, should keep you going far beyond the one hundred days!

TODAY'S PRAYER

Ask God to bring back the initial thrill, joy, and expectancy that you had at your first hearing of the Good News of Jesus. Then let this be the backdrop of your every need and prayer—always.

TODAY'S PROGRESS

_____

_____

_____

_____

_____

_____

_____

_____

_____

The Good, the Bad, and the World

He causes his sun to rise on the evil and the good, and sends rain on the righteous and the unrighteous.

–MATTHEW 5:45

This is one of those proverbial good-news-bad-news statements. We love the idea that God sends good things to us (the good guys) but not that he sends the same good to evil and unworthy people or to people we don't like (the bad guys). But in thinking this, we may have forgotten that he sent many good things our way long before we ever thought about him and his kingdom.

So what's really important here is that God is the way he is, with or without our advice. He's generous and kind even to the ungrateful and wicked (Luke 6:35). Paul says it's God's kindness that is intended to lead people to repentance (Rom. 2:4). If God is deliberately kind to those who either hate him or have no interest in him, then how much more does he pay attention to those who love him and seek his will from day to day!

It's far too easy to underestimate the generosity and goodness of God. When he doesn't give us what we want when we want it, we imagine him callous and miserly. But when we pray, we should keep this in the forefront of our minds: God listens carefully to us and considers our requests with perfect knowledge and intelligence, with incomparable wisdom in what he should grant and not grant, and when.

If something is good for us and the time is right for it, then he comes to us as the God of off-the-charts generosity and lavish blessing. Remember, often it's his generosity and kindness that keep us from getting what we think we want at the moment.

And if your neighbor (the one you think doesn't deserve a single good thing from God) happens to receive a blessing not given to you, then rejoice that there is a God who does such things for the unworthy. If that weren't true, we wouldn't have anything good either.

TODAY'S PRAYER

As you pray, count your blessings for all the wonderful gifts that God has already bestowed on you. Remind him that you desire him and his kingdom even more than all the earthly gifts he brings.

TODAY'S PROGRESS

Money, Money, Money

*Keep your lives free from the love of money and be content
with what you have, because God has said, "Never will I
leave you; never will I forsake you."*

–HEBREWS 13:5

Should we be praying for more money? Isn't it unspiritual
to ask God for the very thing that lies behind so many of
the evils of the world? Money, money, money! It seems like the
whole world goes after it every day, all day long. The mad pursuit of more and more money never ends.

But let's get our theology straight. There's nothing wrong
with money. It's not a "necessary evil." It's not an evil at all. It
can become one, but in itself it is neutral. In fact, every evil we
can name is merely a twist or corruption of some original good.

The real problem with money is not the possession of it
but the love of it, the place it occupies in our hearts. Whenever
it takes on an importance to us greater than God, it becomes
just another idol and leads to all kinds of evils. Whenever we
become overly dependent on our own financial welfare, God
doesn't mind bringing us back to basics. When he does this,
it's for our good.

Nothing touches us so deeply as a crisis of finances. It puts
us on our knees in a big hurry, reminding us that God really
is in charge. God knows how much money we need and often
gives us more than that. But if we pray for more and don't get
it, then we can trust that he will provide in some other way or
that he is training us for some good end.

God often uses money issues to point to the fact that we're completely dependent upon him for everything—every single thing we need in this world. When there isn't enough in the bank or the cupboard, then we come back to this most basic position in life: Whatever the situation, our ultimate source of life and provision is and will always be God. And he is the One who will never leave or forsake us.

TODAY'S PRAYER

Feel completely free to ask God for money or for anything you truly need. Thank him for what he chooses to bring (or not bring), knowing that every move he makes is based on his best plan for you.

TODAY'S PROGRESS

_____

_____

_____

_____

_____

_____

_____

_____

The Journey

To him who is able to keep you from falling and to present
you before his glorious presence without fault and with
great joy—to the only God our Savior be glory, majesty,
power and authority, through Jesus Christ our Lord, before
all ages, now and forevermore! Amen.

–JUDE 1:24–25

In this final blessing, at the end of a little (usually unread) letter at the back of the New Testament, is the entire gospel in a nutshell. It is a power-packed verse that can enter your thinking and produce no end of confidence and enthusiasm for the future, particularly when the future might look pretty grim at the moment.

Don't you ever wonder whether you're really going to make it all the way to the end? Do you ever think of giving up the faith journey because you don't have the strength to keep going or because it's just too hard?

A great part of keeping up prayer in the face of great odds or discouragement is the confidence that things will work out in our favor at the end, and that the end is not in our control anyway. What this little verse is saying is that God finds us just where we are, then picks us up and carries us through life in his protective hands, sustaining us all the way by his own power, then sets us down at the end in his presence as acceptable in his sight. It is he alone who ushers us into his kingdom and presents us before his glorious presence as without fault and with great joy.

God is our Savior through Jesus Christ's work, and it is his doing from first to last. We can't save ourselves or make it easier for him to do it, for he is the author and finisher of the entire program. We will end up in his presence forgiven and received on the basis of his character and his plan for us laid down before the creation of the world.

This is the very heart of the gospel, and it's something that can't be found in any other philosophy or belief system anywhere in the world, in this generation or any other. There's nothing that can be compared to it or even come close. Jesus Christ is our sure foundation, our comfort, and our hope.

TODAY'S PRAYER

As you pray over the long haul, ask God to teach you to relax in his arms knowing that he is busy carrying out his plan to bring you to his everlasting safety and joy.

TODAY'S PROGRESS

_____

_____

_____

_____

_____

_____

_____

The Number of Our Days

All the days ordained for me were written in your book
before one of them came to be.

–PSALM 139:16

This passage states very clearly that God is in charge of our lives and that he is the one who determines the exact number of days we have to live on the earth. Paul says something similar in his sermon at the Areopagus in Athens (Acts 17:26). It is God who sets the boundaries of our lives and the places in which we live them.

Of course to anyone living in denial of God's existence, his sovereignty, and his plan for humanity, this is not exciting at all. Many people just don't want someone in that much control over things. But once again, for the believer this is great news! God oversees our days, counts them one by one, and grants us every beat of our hearts and every breath we breathe. This is true of everyone's heart and everyone's breath, whether we care to acknowledge him or not. He's still the one who determines each and every day. Denying it doesn't change the fact of it.

What this means in practical terms is that not only is the number of our days divinely determined, but what occurs within each one of those days (even up to each second) is no surprise to God. We live securely and under an overarching purpose because our days are in his hands. He was aware of the events of our lives long before we ever came on the scene, and he's not only with us in our joyful times but is also constantly with us through every uphill struggle, pain, sorrow, and loss.

So we can take great pleasure in the clear fact that our lives are running on a track of divine purpose and that the end (*destination*, not just *termination*), guaranteed to us through the resurrection of the Lord Jesus Christ, is a very happy one.

TODAY'S PRAYER

Since only God knows the number of your days, ask him to pack into each day as much of his kingdom as you can possibly contain. Pray that God will cause every single day of your life to count for him.

TODAY'S PROGRESS

In a Name

But in these last days he has spoken to us by his Son, whom
he appointed heir of all things, and through whom he made
the universe. The Son is the radiance of God's glory and the
exact representation of his being, sustaining all things by
his powerful word. After he had provided purification for
sins, he sat down at the right hand of the Majesty in heaven.

–HEBREWS 1:2–3

It's good to remind ourselves as often as possible in whose name we're praying. We need to keep in our minds the nature and credentials of the one who ushers us into God's presence in the first place. Just think about it—Jesus, the entryway into the throne room of the heavenly Father, is the divine Son of God; he was appointed heir of all things and was involved in the creation of the universe; he is the radiance of God's glory and the exact representation of God's being. He sustains all things by his word and sits at the right hand of God where he rules over all things on earth.

He is not just another prophet, an extraordinary man or interesting religious figure. He is the only Son from the Father and was sent to our world to take on human form and live the life that no other human ever did or could. He did everything that needed to be done to secure our salvation and get our lives on earth back on track to fulfill the Creator's original intent.

We are praying in his name, by his authority and by his power, and God hears our prayers because Jesus has paved the way for our access into the presence of God. It is no small matter to pray in Jesus' name, for it releases the greatest power known on earth. Let this fact take center stage: no great event of nature (hurricane, tornado, earthquake, or tsunami) or power of science can even begin to compare with the unimaginable power under the control of Jesus, the Son of God. This power can be unleashed through the simplest prayer of the humblest believer.

Fervent, steadfast prayer in Jesus' name has stopped armies, pulled down empires, changed the course of nations, altered weather, and resulted in revolutions against every form of tyranny. Believe that your prayer has the potential of transforming and renewing your life in the most amazing ways to the glory of God.

TODAY'S PRAYER

As you are praying in the name of Jesus, always remember the indescribable glory of his stature and power. Pray that God will not permit you to fall for the world's desperate and unceasing attempt to lower him in your eyes.

TODAY'S PROGRESS

_____

_____

_____

_____

_____

_____

Where Our Help Comes From

I lift up my eyes to the hills—where does my help come from?
My help comes from the LORD, the Maker of heaven and earth.
He will not let your foot slip—he who watches over you will
not slumber; indeed, he who watches over Israel will neither
slumber nor sleep. The LORD watches over you—the LORD is
your shade at your right hand; the sun will not harm you by
day, nor the moon by night. The LORD will keep you from all
harm—he will watch over your life; the LORD will watch over
your coming and going both now and forevermore.

—PSALM 121

The security and sense of safety and well-being that come from the all-protective, superhuman guardian who never dozes or sleeps are the greatest things that could ever be on this earth. We live in a time when too many have fallen for the false notion that the healthy and mature person is someone who can go it alone, who can stand against the winds of life without "some cosmic crutch" or illusion of a mythical, heavenly grandfather.

But many generations of strong, healthy people have lived and thrived under the knowledge that all of life is lived on the king's property, that there is no one who really "goes it alone," and that every breath we breathe and every beat of the heart is a gift from our heavenly Father. Every day we live is granted to us one by one by someone in charge of the universe who loves us and intends to watch over us.

Most of us are slow learners in this respect. When we are young, we tend to imagine that we survived those close calls, last second rescues, and near-death experiences due to just plain good luck or because of our cleverness or quick thinking. But as the years go by and we gain a clearer view of things, we begin to see that there must have been some intelligent, rational being and power behind all those things. The simple explanation of "coincidence" wears pretty thin after the number of experiences mounts up.

The person who fully understands the physical and spiritual perils of this life, yet rests in the confidence that all is (and will be) well, is the one who sees life through the lenses of the psalmist. Our help comes from the Maker of heaven and earth. Here is the basis of our hope and the reason we can hold our head up high and go forward with confidence.

TODAY'S PRAYER

Never stop praying that God will deliver you from our human temptation—namely, to think that we are somehow responsible for all the good things that come our way. Remember to thank God for his extravagant grace shown to you from your first day to your last.

TODAY'S PROGRESS

_____

_____

_____

_____

The Right Stuff

*Blessed is the man who perseveres under trial, because
when he has stood the test, he will receive the crown of life
that God has promised to those who love him.*

–JAMES 1:12

When understood in one way, this passage becomes very good news; but if it is misunderstood, it's the height of bad news. Here's the bad news first: some people imagine that God blesses whoever is able to "gut it out," the one who can "hang in there" by sheer self-discipline and inner determination to get through life, like the athlete who endures years of unbelievable pain just to get to the Olympics. So to those who have successfully passed the hard test, the reward is coming. They think the "test" is designed to see if they've got the right stuff in them.

As I said, this is the bad news. Why? Because it carries within it this meaning: "God helps those who help themselves." The problem is that most of us realize that the right stuff is *not* in us. We don't have the goods to get there. We're not equipped to drive ourselves to the goal line. Rather, we're beset with weaknesses and frailties, doubts and fears of all sorts. So we'll never be strong enough or good enough to get the crown. Our sins will eventually cause us to fall by the wayside.

So what's the answer? The good news! And the good news in this passage becomes clear by a wider reading of all the New Testament. When we get the big picture, all kinds of things open up to us. See it this way: The "test" that God designs for us believers is not primarily to see if we already have the right stuff in us but to put the right stuff in us. The purpose of the test is to equip us for the journey and to supply what we don't already have.

So the "crown" (reward) is for those God loves enough to discipline, who are called out of their self-reliance and self-sufficiency to the sufficiency of God. He first puts in us the desire to pass the test, then enables and empowers us to pass it, then rewards us for passing it. Isn't that the best news you've ever heard?

TODAY'S PRAYER

Do you get discouraged by your failure to live up to your personal expectations of how good you should be? Ask the Holy Spirit to write upon your heart with indelible ink the message that it's not you but he who can make it happen.

TODAY'S PROGRESS

Hopes and Dreams

Commit to the LORD whatever you do, and your
plans will succeed.

–PROVERBS 16:3

This is an interesting proverb. It isn't an absolute blanket promise that God will always make our personal plans succeed as long as we just run them by him first, as so many people mistakenly think. That would be chaos! No, this is a piece of wisdom that encourages us to commit and submit all our business, activities, and plans to God so that if they are good and in line with his highest will, they'll come to fruition.

This proverb means that true success on this earth depends on our Maker, and if we're to see anything come of our lives, we need to live under the watchful eye and guidance of our heavenly parent. We all want success in what we do, and we all seek to avoid failure. God wants us to know that he's not against our success (he's actually for it); it's just that our efforts should tie in to the overall plan and purposes he has for us and for those around us.

History is full of accounts of people who submitted their hopes and dreams to God before pursuing them and who wanted their plans to honor God above everything else. Before Eric Liddell began his career as a missionary to China, he dreamed of success as a sprinter as a way of honoring God. He made a personal vow never to run on the Lord's Day, and the day came when he was faced with the choice of either running on a Sunday or not participating in the Olympic Games in Paris, France. He chose to forfeit the Olympics instead of breaking his vow. But as things worked out, his decision led to running another race on another day in which he took not only the gold medal but also set a world record, bringing great honor not only to himself but to his God and his homeland.

So if you feel that your plans are good and in line with what you think God has led you to do, submit them to him. If after you do, everything seems to fall apart, don't get discouraged. Wait on him to do something unexpected and far better than you could ever imagine. Sometimes you will know immediately how much more blessing there is in his plans for you; sometimes it might take longer. Just don't give up hope—wait on God. In time (his time) you'll see it.

TODAY'S PRAYER

Pray today for the patience to stand firm while it appears that nothing whatsoever is happening in response to your prayers. It's only appearance.

TODAY'S PROGRESS

_____

_____

_____

_____

_____

_____

_____

It Will Pass Away

Do not fret because of evil men or be envious of those
who do wrong; for like the grass they will soon wither,
like green plants they will soon die away. Trust in the
LORD and do good; dwell in the land and enjoy safe
pasture. Delight yourself in the LORD and he will give
you the desires of your heart.

−PSALM 37:1−4

These first verses put in a nutshell for us the impact of the entire psalm. (I encourage you to re-read it several times and see.) David speaks in many of his psalms of people who for one reason or another wanted him humiliated, beaten down, or dead. There seemed to be no shortage of them. They weren't merely disagreeable antagonists: they were downright evil, and they wanted something really terrible to befall him. Like David, so often in life we bump up against the same type of people.

But David insists that we should never be brought down by their malice toward us. Rather we should just trust God, go about our business and do what is right, and in time they will simply vanish. We'll look around, and they won't be there. Gone. Out of sight.

We shouldn't even fret ourselves over them or be envious of them. They have nothing we want, and what seems to be success in their evil plans is merely appearance and is entirely temporary. It's God's job to take care of them in his time, so we ought not even allow ourselves to stress over them.

This encouragement comes straight out of not merely

David's experience but also that of his ancestors who trusted God for their deliverance. It's also the testimony of the countless people since his day who discovered the same thing. My family and I can add an "amen" to this. Whenever we have placed our hateful opponents into God's hands and just moved on to do our work, wonderful things have happened. We didn't have to lift a finger. He did it all. In fact, our attempts to fix the problems just made things worse.

Our job description remains the same as it was for David. If such are the circumstances that you are praying about, then remember that what we are called upon to do is "trust in the Lord and do good; dwell in the land and enjoy safe pasture."

How hard is that?

TODAY'S PRAYER

Ask God to grant his inexplicable peace of mind even in the hottest fire of resistance or antagonism on the part of others. Remember, it's God's job to take care of them. He will. Just wait and see.

TODAY'S PROGRESS

Where Is Your God?

Why are you downcast, O my soul? Why so disturbed within me? Put your hope in God, for I will yet praise him, my Savior and my God.

–PSALM 42:5–6

David was talking to himself again. Generally not a good sign! But it does sound familiar, doesn't it? I've been there, and you probably have too. Verse three of this psalm really catches my attention: "My tears have been my food day and night, while men say to me all day long, 'Where is your God?'"

But David doesn't allow himself the luxury of wallowing in his tears in terminal self-pity. He reminds himself ("his soul") to put his hope in God, for he looks forward to the moment when he will praise God for his deliverance. He expects it to happen.

There's no doubt in his mind where his help will come from: his Savior and his God. If he (and others) had not experienced fantastic rescues and happy deliverances in life, then there would be no psalms for us to read. Not only would there have been no one to write them, just as importantly, there would have been nothing to write about!

Think about it. There was plenty to do in the ancient world besides writing songs and poetry. Things like, say, survival. It was a rough-and-tumble world with plenty of enemies and dangers. Often the question of the day was, "Will I get through this? Will I be alive by sunset?" So people didn't write such things as we find in the psalms for no reason.

But what a great legacy of information! We have in our hands a book of "family history" telling us how our ancestors of faith faced and conquered all the fresh fears and challenges that arose day by day. It will be the same for us and will give us something to tell our children and grandchildren about.

TODAY'S PRAYER

Pray that when God finally delivers you or answers your prayer, he'll do it in such a way that you can pass on the experience to the next generation. Like you, they'll need all the stories of God's faithfulness they can get.

TODAY'S PROGRESS

_____

_____

_____

_____

_____

_____

_____

_____

_____

_____

Yet . . .

We have heard with our ears, O God; our fathers have told
us what you did in their days, in days long ago. With your
hand you drove out the nations and planted our fathers;
you crushed the peoples and made our fathers flourish. It
was not by their sword that they won the land, nor did their
arm bring them victory; it was your right hand, your arm,
and the light of your face, for you loved them.

–PSALM 44:1–3

What was so unique about the faith of the Hebrews was that they never forgot their history. They first heard about it from their parents when they were small, and they passed on the good news to their children. It was God and God alone who delivered them from the hands of their enemies (who were many) and made them flourish in a new land.

It was God's right hand, his arm of strength, and the light of his face that kept them safe and well, simply because he loved them. Why? We'll never know. They betrayed him and rebelled against him every chance they got. They flaunted his law in his face time after time and did so with great gusto and often very minimal (if any) guilt afterwards.

Yet (yet!—this is the great word hanging over all Hebrew history) God still loved them, subdued their enemies, and led them repeatedly to health and safety. Certainly it was not because they were so good or behaved so honorably but because he loved them with an everlasting love. It was a love that was grounded in his mercy and grace, not in any way in their worthiness to receive it.

So it is with us. Are you having trouble right now asking God for something because you think you don't deserve it or haven't lived the kind of life that would lend itself to his blessing? You're right! You (we) never will. But that's the good news. That's the gospel. God wants to bless and keep us as he did his people of old. Yes, he wants us to be sorry for it all, to repent and turn from all that offends him, and all of that. Absolutely. But what he wants and waits for most of all is to pour out his mercy and favor upon us. Just ask.

TODAY'S PRAYER

Ask the Lord to remove finally and forever the wrong-headed idea that he bases his grace upon our goodness. This idea will trip you up every time you pray. Now thank him once more for the way he is.

TODAY'S PROGRESS

_____

_____

_____

_____

_____

_____

_____

Renewing Our Strength

*Do you not know? Have you not heard? The LORD is the
everlasting God, the Creator of the ends of the earth.
He will not grow tired or weary, and his understanding
no one can fathom. He gives strength to the weary and
increases the power of the weak. Even youths grow tired
and weary, and young men stumble and fall; but those
who hope in the LORD will renew their strength. They
will soar on wings like eagles; they will run and not grow
weary, they will walk and not be faint.*

–ISAIAH 40:28–31

These are encouraging words to anyone who feels beaten and burnt out by life and its unrelenting pressures and problems. Do you feel like things never let up? Troubles keep coming day after day after day, and they even seem to renew their strength during the night as we sleep. Evil never grows tired or gives up. Its energy seems to increase with each passing year. But ours doesn't, and there comes a day when we just can't run against the wind anymore.

This is where God comes in. He is the only true and lasting source of energy and strength. He remains as powerful and full of vitality and life as he was the day he made the universe. He knows that we are going to run out of steam in a hurry. He knows we will end up in desperate need for more strength, more speed, more endurance, more energy, more patience, more faith, and more of everything else just to get through the day—to keep going and complete the course.

When we're young, we think we can handle anything, only to find out later that life isn't ordered that way. But it is in these trials where we finally begin to learn that we were never intended to go it alone or to depend upon ourselves to get there. Life reminds us that "they who hope in the Lord will renew their strength." Nothing will overtake them; nothing will be too overwhelming for them.

We begin to understand that we are supposed to grow tired and weary, we are supposed to stumble and fall, because that's the only way we get the point of our inadequacy and God's all-encompassing sufficiency. It's then we turn to rest in the power and strength of God. As the Lord taught the apostle Paul, "My grace is sufficient for you, for my power is made perfect in weakness" (2 Cor. 12:9).

TODAY'S PRAYER

Ask God continually for more strength, more energy, more of everything it takes to get there in one piece. He never gets tired of hearing that request even when we are weary of making it.

TODAY'S PROGRESS

_____

_____

_____

_____

_____

God Reigns

Hallelujah! For our Lord God Almighty reigns.

–REVELATION 19:6

We pray to God because we believe he has the power and the will to hear us and answer us. We know he has the power to do things for us because he's in a position to overrule other powers and authorities both on earth and in the spiritual realm. That's what it means to say that the Lord God Almighty reigns. He's the ruling king, the highest of the high, the Supreme Judge presiding over the supreme court of the universe. As such, he's the ruler of history—ours and everyone else's.

What's the connection between this point and our prayers? It's the wonderful good news behind all the Bible language: God reigns! He's on his heavenly throne guaranteeing us that righteousness and justice, everything that is good and pure, meaningful and eternal, will be part of the final word spoken over his creation. Whatever is happening today that is prompting our prayers of petition, whatever is causing anxiety or distress, or fear of tomorrow, it is purely temporary and will in time give way to the vibrant life and joy that mark his kingdom.

If there's any doubt that this verse holds encouragement for us in very hard times, then just check the context in which it appears. Everything leading up to it describes the ultimate evil and terror that could ever occur on earth. Death, war, destruction, and pestilence are all around and seem utterly out of control. But even then, the writer tells us, God reigns over and above it all. They can't do a single thing that goes beyond God's permission.

So whatever our situation or level of desperation, we pray with this hope: God will bring to us our bread for today, all that we need, and will sustain us every day thereafter both in this world and the next. Never forget it, never doubt it ... God reigns!

TODAY'S PRAYER

Pray that the Holy Spirit will do what only he can do—teach you how to enjoy the fact that God reigns over everything, even when all appearances are to the contrary.

TODAY'S PROGRESS

_____

_____

_____

_____

_____

_____

_____

_____

_____

_____

Forget About the Past

*Forget the former things; do not dwell on the past. See,
I am doing a new thing! Now it springs up; do you
not perceive it? I am making a way in the desert and
streams in the wasteland.*

–ISAIAH 43:18–19

This is another of those passages where God is explaining to
Israel that, even though they have acted disgracefully and
been profoundly unfaithful to him, he is still faithful to them
and intends to restore all that was lost when they turned away
from his goodness.

So the promise is clearly not to those who have performed
so excellently along the way and are now being congratulated for
it, but rather it's for those who have completely fumbled the ball
and come up badly beaten. It's the kind of astonishing promise
he gives to all of us who can't claim a single credit in God's eyes,
who have nothing to offer him except our sins and failures, and
who deserve to end up with nothing but are given everything.

It's a way of saying, "Now stop dwelling on the stupidities
and mistakes of your past because I'm going to blot out all that
and make a new way for you. You're in the desert wasteland
right now, but I'm going to order just for you streams in your
desert place and create an oasis where there was only dry sand
and no hope of ever finding your way out." Just a few verses
later, God puts it this way: "I, even I, am he who blots out your
transgressions, for my own sake, and remembers your sins no
more" (Isa. 43:25).

We live in a day of endless homemade you-get-what-you-pay-for theologies and Bible teachers who try to persuade us that the gospel is about the level and quality of our faith and performance. Get better, try harder, and God will reward you! But the end of all such thinking about God is despair since we know deep down that we just can't do it on our own. The best we can do is fall short.

Why does God insist on giving us this kind of hope and rescue when we have given him nothing but rebellion and foolishness? Just because that's who God is—the Holy One of Israel. It's the mark of his character, and by that alone and nothing else we are sure of our happy destiny.

TODAY'S PRAYER

Pray that God will do that new thing for you. Ask him to open a door that doesn't even now exist, or create a way out that you can't possibly imagine. God loves to make a way *ex nihilo* (out of nothing).

TODAY'S PROGRESS

_____

_____

_____

_____

_____

_____

The Main Plot

In him we have redemption through his blood, the
forgiveness of sins, in accordance with the riches of
God's grace that he lavished on us with all wisdom and
understanding. And he made known to us the mystery of
his will according to his good pleasure, which he purposed
in Christ, to be put into effect when the times will have
reached their fulfillment—to bring all things in heaven and
on earth together under one head, even Christ.

—EPHESIANS 1:7–10

This passage comes as close to any other in the Bible to giving a thumbnail sketch of what it's all about. It's the main plot revealed. It's the summary of what everything is here for. It puts in capsule form the meaning of creation, the entire history of the earth and the human race, the story of the Bible, and everything else up to and beyond the last day of the world as we know it. It gives us a cutaway view of the destination of the world and reveals all the hidden mechanisms operating behind the scenes.

There is a counterpart to this in the Old Testament. Chapters 40 to 55 of Isaiah describe the goal of all history. In particular, Isaiah 40:5 tells us that this goal is the revelation of God's glory to the whole world.

In other words, God is moving all things everywhere toward the final disclosure of his glory to all living beings: the uniting in Jesus Christ of persons, nations, dreams, and projects. He will be the focal point of every last thing in creation as each piece is brought into line with the will of the Father.

What will that look like? We can't imagine it totally because we've never seen anything like it. But having said that, we can still begin to envision it by remembering the best and happiest moments of life we've ever lived, putting together the highest and best dreams we've ever had. Add to that: productive work that is all pleasure, adventure without peril, unending exploration, sport, feasting, friendship and love that never disappoint, and, best of all, the presence and supervision of a loving God who ever continues to create for the creatures he loves.

With the promise of that before us, what could possibly trip us up? We can get through anything this world throws us as we press on toward the goal.

TODAY'S PRAYER

In the monotony of daily life, are you tempted to lose heart or lose the vision of what the whole thing is about? Ask for a renewal of the big picture in the center of your being. It'll dwarf the thing you face today.

TODAY'S PROGRESS

_____

_____

_____

_____

_____

_____

By His Spirit

"Not by might nor by power, but by my Spirit,"
*says the L*ORD *Almighty.*

—ZECHARIAH 4:6

Countless preachers and missionaries have launched their ministries with this passage as their life theme. It's pretty straightforward. God tells his people through the prophet Zechariah that if they're going to accomplish anything in his name, it will be not on their own strength or through human devices but by the power of his Spirit. And this is exactly what people have found through the ages.

Probably most of us step out in our early years of faith imagining that with our training, expertise, money, or whatever, we can move the kingdom forward and accomplish quite well what God wants us to do. But we quickly learn the first lesson of faith—we all must complete Christian Life 101 before we're of any use to God!

If we don't get this one right, we won't do a single thing of any lasting value. It is by the power of God and his wisdom, not ours, that something important and pleasing to God is done. He can; we can't. He will; we won't. Often he allows us to try and fail just so that we'll get the point. The worse our failure, the clearer and longer lasting the lesson. But if he does allow us to fail miserably, it's not to humiliate us but to teach us that he will do great things through us if we'll just let him.

So let's let God be God. Trying to do God's job for him is just too much work and far too stressful. We were never intended to try. But what a relief and joy for us when we start to see things happen through his power. Joyful, fulfilling ministry begins to take place when we realize that God is not the genie in our bottle but, rather, we are the obedient instruments in his hands.

TODAY'S PRAYER

Ask God to show you what he wants to teach you through what you are facing, and to use you for his good purpose because of it.

TODAY'S PROGRESS

_____

_____

_____

_____

_____

_____

_____

_____

_____

_____

_____

_____

Our Growing Faith

Be still, and know that I am God; I will be exalted among
the nations, I will be exalted in the earth.

−PSALM 46:10

The psalmist's words are an echo of those of Moses when he stood near the Red Sea with the approaching Egyptian army on one side and the sea on the other. When the Hebrews stood on the shore looking at the two options of either drowning on the one hand or being recaptured and enslaved by the cruel Egyptians, they were filled with fear. Moses reassured them with the command to stand firm, be still, and allow God to do what only he can do (Ex. 14:13–14).

If there's something that God wants us to learn above everything else in life, it's this: we are not nor can we be in charge of our destiny. In most of the great crises and turning points in life, our task is not to attempt to fix or save ourselves but to be still in expectant faith and wait for the deliverance of God. It is God and God alone who will be exalted among the nations of the earth.

If you've tried everything else under the sun and still can't get yourself a single inch out of the hole, then realize that God has put you into one of those places where he intends to create total dependence upon him and wants full credit for your rescue. It will happen in God's time—when he has squeezed every last ounce of faith-stretching value out of your circumstance.

TODAY'S PRAYER

Have you tried everything you can to fix the circumstance you're facing? Take the time today just to be still before God and know that he can do what we cannot.

TODAY'S PROGRESS

Joy

If you obey my commands, you will remain in my love, just as I have obeyed my Father's commands and remain in his love. I have told you this so that my joy may be in you and that your joy may be complete.

−JOHN 15:10−11

Jesus doesn't leave us on our own to figure out how to please and serve him and God the Father. He gives us the game plan to move forward successfully. Just as he obeyed on earth the directions of his Father, so we are to follow his lead as well. It's our obedience to him that keeps us dwelling in his love and on track toward the kingdom, and he leads us by his Spirit into right living one day at a time.

In reading this gospel, you might have realized that there are very few recorded commands of Jesus. So what does he mean when he talks about obeying his commands? It looks as though he wants us to understand that, in our mysterious connection with him and the Father, he will reveal his commands to us day by day. The closer we get to him, the more and clearer will be his commands, directions, and course corrections.

What's the end result of this kind of life in love? Joy! Where the Spirit of Jesus is, there's joy. It is the most visible token of Jesus' presence! This joy manifests itself in loving and practical ways. When we reach out and place others before us, then we live in joy.

It's in this joy that we remain positive and work confidently toward the gleaming brightness of his coming kingdom, knowing that he will bless, rescue, and save us when the time is right.

Equally important is this key point: it's only the joy people see in us that will make a lasting impression. True joy is a very rare commodity in this world, and people will sit up and take notice when they see it. Do you want to reflect the kingdom of God? Then let Jesus' joy reign in your life.

TODAY'S PRAYER

As you pray, ask God to grant you the joy that only he can bring, no matter how bleak things may look at the moment.

TODAY'S PROGRESS

_____

_____

_____

_____

_____

_____

_____

_____

_____

_____

The Final Chapter

"He will wipe every tear from their eyes. There will be
no more death or mourning or crying or pain, for the old
order of things has passed away."

–REVELATION 21:4

This is the perfect conclusion to the entire Bible. It's the last act of the play, the amazing final chapter of the mystery story begun in the first few chapters of Genesis. Just as heaven and earth were linked together at the beginning of history, so that God's presence was at the same time a paradise for humans and animals on earth, so it will be restored in a similar but far greater way at the end.

When sin and rebellion entered the world at the beginning, the perfect communion humans had with God and the perfect unity and peace enjoyed by all life on earth came to an end. The story of life thereafter is but the long and sorrowful record of fallen human life and all the chaos, foolishness, and blindness ever since.

The story could have ended there. Happily, it didn't. It continues with a God who refuses to abandon his fallen and prodigal world, a God of steadfast love and faithfulness that exceeds all boundaries and even reason. It ends with a restoration of all that was lost and with a conclusion that's even better than the beginning. Heaven returns to kiss the earth and transform it all into the likeness of the perfect heavenly kingdom. God himself appears on the scene again to rule in person over his beloved creation and to banish forever all evil, tears, pain, bitterness, and death. Paradise is restored. And that is God's last word pronounced over our universe.

On this day of our special one hundred days of prayer, just remember that whatever comes our way from this day forward is not a picture of our final state. Wherever we are, pleasant or painful, it's just another campsite along the way toward the great city of God. All pain, disillusionment, failure, distress, disappointment, and loss are but temporary stages that some-day won't even be a memory.

When you know your destination, you can get through the bad stretches along the way. And since the God who will bring his kingdom to us at the end is with us every minute of the day now, we have every reason to expect a great deal of good to come our way as we continue to ask, seek, and knock.

TODAY'S PRAYER

Knowing what the ultimate end looks like and who it is who will bring it to pass (and your security in it all), pray now that God will bring as much of his heaven to earth as possible through you to others.

TODAY'S PROGRESS

A New Day

Now to him who is able to do immeasurably more than all
we ask or imagine, according to his power that is at work
within us, to him be glory in the church and in Christ Jesus
throughout all generations, for ever and ever! Amen.

–EPHESIANS 3:20–21

Here is one of the greatest blessings in the Bible. It follows after some of the highest promises and truths in it. It answers the question, "How can we ever get anything done for God in a world where it seems like everything is against us?"

This is what gets us out of bed in the morning so we can stand against the tidal wave of opposition or thick lead wall of indifference. Remember, this statement comes from a man who lived twenty-four hours a day, seven days a week, in the midst of the most terrible conditions and in a generation that clung to every other religion or philosophy under the sun except Jesus.

It rarely appears to be the case that God will accomplish something greater than what we can ask or imagine, because the odds against us are so great. It's like standing on the beach watching a two-hundred-foot tsunami coming at us from the sea. Our puny efforts or good intentions seem pretty feeble compared to the overwhelming opposition ahead of us.

But what we need to get straight once and for all is that our own personal measurement of things is totally irrelevant when it comes to our labor in the kingdom of God. It really doesn't matter what it looks like or how insignificant we think we are. It's not about us. It's about God and his power. What he wants of us is not our spectacular talents or great ability to be success-ful. He wants our faithfulness. He takes care of the rest.

In the end, we aren't responsible for the success of our efforts or the timing of it. If we'll just do what he puts in front of us, he'll produce what he wants in his time and way.

On our one hundredth day of prayer, let us rededicate our-selves, our families, our resources, our lives—all that we are and have—to the glory and honor of God. Let us commit ourselves to exhibiting his love and compassion and to letting him do with us whatever pleases him and best fulfills his plans for our lives. It's the only thing we can do in this life that's really worth it.

TODAY'S PRAYER

Since only the things we do in the name of Jesus can never be in vain, let us pray that whatever our need, may God use us (as well as our need) as instruments for his great program of his-tory, far exceeding what we can ask or imagine.

TODAY'S PROGRESS

_____

_____

_____

_____

_____

_____

_____

God of the
Last Minute

Whether we study the Bible, the history of Israel, or the church, there's a consistent theme that reappears in each: God likes to take his time in doing his will, but he's never late in doing it. This means that often (very often) God prefers to wait until the last minute, the fifty-ninth minute of the eleventh hour, to answer our prayers and bring about his will and purposes.

That God likes to do it this way is not hard to prove. Just read the hundreds of books written by Christians throughout the ages describing this characteristic of God. God lets us wait and wait (and wait some more) until the very last second before opening up the door or catching us in our fall.

But why? It may seem like unnecessary drama to us, but it seems to fit God's character and historical pattern perfectly. What we can all notice after going through one of these spiritual roller-coaster rides is this: it's in those last moments or hours of expectant waiting that our faith takes on new dimensions. We are being stretched as we near the end.

If God answered our prayers of desperation the very moment we prayed (which he sometimes does), it's likely we wouldn't grow very much. But if God lets us hang on in fervent prayer for an extended period of time, causing us to recognize that we are totally dependent upon him and not ourselves, then he accomplishes something he doesn't in another way.

Also, because of our fallen, disobedient nature, there's something about us that we are very slow to admit. When we find our own way out of some kind of trouble, we tend to think it was really thanks to our own skill or cleverness. If there is the slightest doubt that it might have been God who helped us, we usually lean toward self-congratulation rather than humble praise and thankful submission to our Rescuer.

But if God waits until the very last second, after allowing every possible attempt on our part to get ourselves out of the jam, then we are more apt to see the divine hand in the whole business. God chooses this path for many of us because he wants us to recognize his perfect plan and purpose for our lives.

In such life experiences, the Creator makes his favorite point once again: "I'm God, and you aren't. I am in charge of your life, and you aren't. I have a purpose for your life, and now it's time for you to pay attention!"

So the next time God takes his own sweet time in coming your way, just thank him for making his presence known and clear, for doing it his way, and for training you to meet the challenge ahead. Just say yes to his call to serve him. Abandon your own private kingdom and follow him into his.

CONCLUDING DATE

_____

HOW GOD ANSWERED MY PRAYER

"Lord, as I reflect on my one hundred days of prayer . . ."

_____

_____

_____

A FINAL PRAYER

Lord, as I reflect on my one hundred days of prayer, I realize more than ever before that I'm totally and forever dependent upon you and your mercy. It's not the quality or the quantity of my words that unite your will and mine. It's not my goodness, faithfulness, or great spiritual performance that make the difference but, rather, your goodness and unearned faithfulness toward me. So in spite of all I've asked for and the many times I've repeated to you my desires and wishes, and as strongly as I want what I want, what I really desire above all else is your highest and best. I pray with and in the name of your Son Jesus: let your perfect will alone be done. Amen.

ABOUT THE AUTHOR

Dr. John I. Snyder is a pastor, author, and conference speaker. He has taught New Testament Studies at New College Berkeley, California, and has pastored and planted churches in California, New York, and Switzerland.

John received his Bachelor of Arts from Vanguard University (Costa Mesa, California), his Master of Theology and Master of Divinity degrees from Princeton Theological Seminary, and his Doctor of Theology from the University of Basel, Switzerland.

He has contributed articles to *Theology Today*, *Dialog*, *Theologische Zeitschrift*, *Journal of the Evangelical Theological Society*, *The Washington Times*, and others. John has also served on the adjunct faculty of New College Berkeley as well as the World Journalism Institute. He is the founder of community321.com, an online faith community discussing God, church, religion, and everything in between.

Currently, John is organizing church planting in Europe with his wife, Shirin, and two daughters, Sarah and Stephanie.